Racial and Ethnic Discrimination

ISSUES

Volume 172

Series Editor

Lisa Firth

Independence

Educational Publishers
Cambridge

First published by Independence
The Studio, High Green
Great Shelford
Cambridge CB22 5EG
England

© Independence 2009

British Library Cataloguing in Publication Data
Racial and Ethnic Discrimination – (Issues; v. 172)
1. Racism
I. Series II. Firth, Lisa
305.8-dc22

ISBN-13: 978 1 86168 486 8

Printed in Great Britain
MWL Print Group Ltd

Cover
The illustration on the front cover is by
Simon Kneebone.

CONTENTS

Chapter One: Racial Discrimination

Chapter Two: Ethnicity and Identity

Useful information for readers

Dear Reader,

Issues: Racial and Ethnic Discrimination

Britain is a multiracial society, with 63% of people in a recent survey saying that they mixed with others from a different ethnic or religious background socially. However, discrimination is still experienced by many of those belonging to minority ethnic and religious groups. What are the causes of racial intolerance, and how can it be tackled? This title examines the issues.

The purpose of *Issues*

Racial and Ethnic Discrimination is the one hundred and seventy-second volume in the **Issues** series. The aim of this series is to offer up-to-date information about important issues in our world. Whether you are a regular reader or new to the series, we do hope you find this book a useful overview of the many and complex issues involved in the topic. This title replaces an older volume in the **Issues** series, Volume 115: **Racial Discrimination,** which is now out of print.

Titles in the **Issues** series are resource books designed to be of especial use to those undertaking project work or requiring an overview of facts, opinions and information on a particular subject, particularly as a prelude to undertaking their own research.

The information in this book is not from a single author, publication or organisation; the value of this unique series lies in the fact that it presents information from a wide variety of sources, including:

⇨ Government reports and statistics
⇨ Newspaper articles and features
⇨ Information from think-tanks and policy institutes
⇨ Magazine features and surveys
⇨ Website material
⇨ Literature from lobby groups and charitable organisations. *

Critical evaluation

Because the information reprinted here is from a number of different sources, readers should bear in mind the origin of the text and whether the source is likely to have a particular bias or agenda when presenting information (just as they would if undertaking their own research). It is hoped that, as you read about the many aspects of the issues explored in this book, you will critically evaluate the information presented. It is important that you decide whether you are being presented with facts or opinions. Does the writer give a biased or an unbiased report? If an opinion is being expressed, do you agree with the writer?

Racial and Ethnic Discrimination offers a useful starting point for those who need convenient access to information about the many issues involved. However, it is only a starting point. Following each article is a URL to the relevant organisation's website, which you may wish to visit for further information.

Kind regards,

Lisa Firth
Editor, **Issues** series

*Please note that Independence Publishers has no political affiliations or opinions on the topics covered in the **Issues** series, and any views quoted in this book are not necessarily those of the publisher or its staff.*

Frequently asked questions

Information from Show Racism the Red Card

What is race?

In the past, people believed that there were different races of people, who shared common physical features such as skin colour, hair type, facial features, character and skills. Racists have used this idea to label certain 'races' as fundamentally different and inferior.

However, we now know through genetics that there is just one species to which we all belong and that people of all colours and appearances have a similar potential. The physical differences between people around the world are external, not internal, and are caused by the adaptation of people over long periods of time to different environments.

The genes that code for our physical appearance are a very small number and are not in any way connected to genes which code for other characteristics. The genetic differences between so-called races are smaller than the differences within these groups.

What is racism?

Though race is an arbitrary social concept, racism is very real. Racism is the belief that people who have a different skin colour, nationality or culture are inferior. Racist ideas have developed over thousands of years and have been used to justify the oppression of many different groups of people.

What forms does racism take?

Racism can take many forms, ranging from verbal abuse to outright physical attacks on a person or property. Racism can also be non-verbal, for example denying a person from a minority ethnic background a job or entry to a restaurant or shop, purely on the grounds of their colour, nationality or religion. This is known as race discrimination and is illegal.

There is also 'institutional racism'. This is when an organisation's procedures and policies amount to disadvantaging people from minority ethnic backgrounds. It is defined by the Stephen Lawrence Inquiry as 'the collective failure of an organisation to provide an appropriate and professional service to people because of their colour, culture or ethnic origin. It can be seen or detected in processes, attitudes and behaviour which amount to discrimination through unwitting prejudice, ignorance, thoughtlessness and racial stereotyping which disadvantages minority ethnic people.'

To combat this type of racism, laws have been put in place to try and ensure that bodies like schools, universities, hospitals, the police, government departments and local councils take action (pro-active rather than reactive) to make sure they are not discriminating against people from minority ethnic backgrounds, whether they are employees or members of the public. This will help to ensure that public services meet everyone's needs.

Why is racism wrong?

Racism is wrong because it judges a person and their capabilities based on a very limited set of categories, such as religion or nationality. This leads to a lack of understanding and segregation of peoples and cultures. It also encourages hostility towards any person of a different background. Racism teaches people to hate each other purely on the basis of skin colour, nationality or culture, even though we are all of one race – the human race. It is much better to live in a multicultural society: just think of the things that would be removed from British culture if we lived in a segregated society – e.g. different types of music, food and clothing. Historically, racism has been used to separate and segregate people of different skin colour, for example under the apartheid regime in South Africa, which ended in 1994, and has also formed the basis for justifying atrocious genocides such as the Holocaust of World War Two.

Many people's lives are seriously affected by racism and discrimination every day, and not just because of verbal or physical abuse. Many people

from minority ethnic backgrounds are not getting the same opportunities as others, whether it is in jobs, education or access to health services or affordable housing. That clearly isn't fair or right as everyone should be given the same opportunities in life.

Why is using the words 'Paki' or 'Chinky' wrong?

Although seen by some as abbreviations for 'Pakistani' and 'Chinese', these words have often been used as terms of abuse and are often accompanied by swear words or insults. Therefore they are extremely offensive and it is not acceptable to use these terms to describe a person who is of Pakistani or Chinese origin or to describe an establishment run by a person of Pakistani or Chinese origins.

Using these words suggests that a person doesn't think about others as individuals and that they judge people on what they look like or where they come from, rather than who they are. Nobody would like people to make judgements about them just by looking at them.

Also, both words tend to be used generally for Asian people, irrespective of their national origins, such as India or Bangladesh in the case of 'Paki', and Korea or Japan in the case of 'Chinky'. Therefore, as well as being offensive, the terms may not even refer to the correct country. Think about how silly you would look to others if you referred to someone from Germany as Spanish, for example.

Why are people racist?

There are many reasons why people are racist. A lot of a person's attitudes and opinions are formed during childhood. If someone is taught to be racist from an early age, by a family member for example, these attitudes are likely to stick with the person throughout their life. Often, when asked, racists are unable to explain why they hate people of a different skin colour, nationality or culture. Racists commonly use people of different ethnic backgrounds as 'scapegoats' on whom to blame their problems and make sweeping negative generalisations about these groups of people. The racist comment 'They take our jobs and our homes' is one of the most frequently cited 'justifications'

for racism. This is simply not true.

Racism can also be stirred up by the media. Witness recent anti-asylum seeker campaigns run by some of the newspapers in Britain. Constantly running stories about 'bogus' asylum seekers and using emotive language such as a 'flood' of refugees helps to create an atmosphere of hostility amongst sections of the general public. Britain is in tenth place in Europe per head of population for asylum applications. The vast majority of refugees go to countries in the Middle East or Africa, often the countries that border their own. Asylum seekers in the UK receive only 70% of the amount of income support a UK citizen would receive. Even though many are well educated and highly skilled and would like to contribute to society, they are not allowed to work.

Do white people suffer racism?

People of all different skin colours can have racism directed at them. Racism can be directed at some groups of white people by other Whites – for example, Irish people have suffered from racial discrimination. However, white people in general are not the most common target and certainly receive far less racism than black or Asian people. The most common form of racism against white people in the UK is against asylum seekers, travellers or migrants from Eastern Europe.

Is Islam a threat to Britain?

Archaeological evidence suggests that Muslims have lived in the UK since 760AD and there have been large Muslim communities here for the past 300 years. Every religious book can be interpreted in many ways: the Bible can and so can the Koran. There are extremists in every faith. A handful of Muslim clerics get a lot of media attention, but the vast majority preach a peaceful religion. You cannot blame every Muslim for the actions of a few. Britain has also had Catholic and Anglican terrorism in recent years, but we did not blame every Catholic for every IRA bomb.

What can you do when you are the target of racism?

If you are a school pupil and have verbal racism directed at you, then you

should tell your parents and a teacher. If it is physical violence to your person, make sure you tell a teacher, your parents and as many of your friends as possible. Racists are much weaker when they realise that they do not have the support of many people.

If you are older and come across racism in the workplace, you should tell your employer and friends. Schools and employers have a legal duty to treat all racist incidents seriously and action will be taken. Whatever age you are, if you are physically attacked it is also important to get in touch with the police.

What can you do when you hear racism directed at other people?

If you hear one of your friends being racially abusive towards another person, have the courage to tell them that you think this is wrong. Try asking why they are doing that and, if they are your friend, they will listen to you and hopefully change their behaviour. Try to get them to apologise. If this doesn't work, ask yourself why you are friends with this person. You should also report incidents to teachers and parents, as they will be in a better position to deal with them.

If you hear racism at a football match, take the number of the person's seat and inform a steward or police officer of their behaviour. They should be dealt with by the club: racist chanting is illegal inside football grounds and will lead to the racist being banned from the ground. If they are a season ticket holder they will have their season ticket taken away from them. In Scotland, you should also report any incidents of racism that occur when either playing or watching football to Show Racism the Red Card's Glasgow office: info@ theredcardscotland.org. In England and Wales, a separate organisation called Kick it Out deals with racism within football, so please report such matters to info@kickitout.org

⇨ The above information is reprinted with kind permission from Show Racism the Red Card. Visit www. srtrc.org for more information.
© Show Racism the Red Card

Public attitudes to race and religion in Britain

Information from Ipsos MORI

The Equality and Human Rights Commission (EHRC) is an independent organisation which aims to eliminate discrimination, reduce inequality, and protect human rights. In February, it commissioned Ipsos MORI to run a telephone poll among adults from different ethnic and religious backgrounds living in Great Britain.

The survey aimed to explore how, if at all, public attitudes towards race and religion have changed. It also looked at how the police are perceived in the eyes of the public ten years after the publication of the Macpherson report, which highlighted failings in the police investigation into the murder of black teenager Stephen Lawrence.

Key findings

About half (49%) of the general public are optimistic Britain will be a more tolerant society in ten years' time. This figure increases amongst people from ethnic minorities, with 58% optimistic about the future.

There are relatively high levels of social interaction between races in Great Britain, with over three in five (63%) people saying they mix with people from a different ethnic or religious background socially outside of work or school.

Young people are more likely to mix; 32% of people aged 16 to 24 mix daily compared to 5% of people aged 65 or over.

Younger people from ethnic minority backgrounds are also more positive about improvements in racial tolerance over the last ten years than their older counterparts. 40% of 16- to 24-year-olds from a minority ethnic background think there is more racial tolerance than ten years ago, compared to 25% for those aged 65 or over.

On the day Obama becomes the USA's first black president, just over half of the general public in this country (56%) think it is likely Britain will have a black, Asian or mixed race Prime Minister in the next 10 to 20 years.

The study shows that faith and belief are a more significant source of tension in Britain than race. Three in five (60%) of the general population and two in three (66%) of those in ethnic minority groups think religion is more divisive than race today.

84% of the general population and 90% of ethnic minority communities support the notion that all ethnic groups in Britain should be free to celebrate their different customs and traditions alongside seeking to integrate into the British way of life.

The survey also reveals that concerns about race and immigration have fallen below worries over the economy and unemployment. When people are asked to rank the issues most concerning them about living in Britain today, half (50%) rank the economy highest, followed by 11% citing unemployment and 8% race and immigration issues. Poll findings from last year show race and immigration were the biggest issue (Ipsos MORI Issues Index December 2007).

In terms of attitudes to the police, when asked to consider the police investigation into the murder of Stephen Lawrence, 36% of the public think there would be similar failings today if the police were to investigate such a crime. This rises to over a half (53%) among ethnic minority groups overall, and to 56% among Black African and Caribbeans specifically.

There is strong support for the idea that the police should be representative of the communities they serve, with four in five (80%) of the general public thinking this is important.

The black community is more negative about treatment by the police. Overall, 38% of the black community think they would be treated worse than other races by the police. This is compared to 9% for the population as a whole.

20 January 2009

⇨ The above information is reprinted with kind permission from Ipsos MORI. Visit www.ipsos-mori.com for more information on this and other topics.

© Ipsos MORI

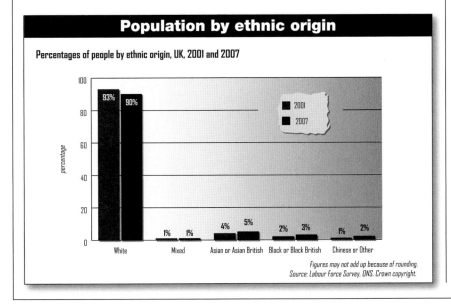

Population by ethnic origin

Percentages of people by ethnic origin, UK, 2001 and 2007

- 2001
- 2007

White: 93% (2001), 90% (2007)
Mixed: 1% (2001), 1% (2007)
Asian or Asian British: 4% (2001), 5% (2007)
Black or Black British: 2% (2001), 3% (2007)
Chinese or Other: 1% (2001), 2% (2007)

Figures may not add up because of rounding.
Source: Labour Force Survey, ONS. Crown copyright.

What is race discrimination?

Information from Your Rights

The Race Relations Act sets out the circumstances in which discrimination on the grounds of race is unlawful. It defines four types of discrimination: direct discrimination, indirect discrimination, victimisation and harassment.

The RRA defines 'racial grounds' as being on the grounds of colour, race, nationality or ethnic or national origins

Direct race discrimination

Direct discrimination occurs when a person treats you less favourably on racial grounds than he or she would treat, or treats, some other person.

The RRA defines 'racial grounds' as being on the grounds of colour, race, nationality or ethnic or national origins. Most people think of race discrimination as being less favourable treatment on the grounds of colour or race. However, discrimination on the grounds of nationality, ethnic or national origins is equally unlawful. Thus if a workplace contains Afro-Caribbean and African employees and the employer treats the African employees less favourably by allocating them the menial or less interesting work, that could amount to less favourable treatment on racial grounds. Similarly, if a Japanese bank offered its services to Korean customers on less favourable terms than those offered to other customers the bank's actions could constitute less favourable treatment on racial grounds.

It is equally unlawful to treat someone less favourably on the grounds of another person's race, so that it is discrimination to treat a white employee less favourably because he or she has a black partner. Similarly, if a white employee were dismissed for refusing to obey his or her employer's instructions to refuse to serve Asian customers, he or she would have a direct discrimination claim under the RRA.

Sometimes direct discrimination is very obvious, but it can be more subtle. The following are all examples of direct discrimination:

⇨ Racist name-calling or abuse.

⇨ Refusing to give someone a job or promote him or her because of stereotyped ideas about his or her abilities or conduct, based on his or her race.

⇨ Refusing to give someone a job or promotion on the grounds that customers will not like being served by a person of that race.

⇨ A pub or club operating quotas to prevent black members or customers from exceeding a specific number or proportion.

Generally, you need to point to someone compared to whom you have been treated less favourably, called a 'comparator'. However, if you cannot do this, the court or tribunal considering your case should construct a hypothetical comparator for you.

The intention and motive of the discriminator are irrelevant to the question of whether a person has been subject to unlawful direct discrimination on the grounds of race. Moreover, race does not need to be the sole or even the principal reason for the way someone is treated for the treatment to be discriminatory. Discrimination can be made out if race is a contributing cause in that it is a 'significant influence' on the treatment in question.

Segregation on racial grounds is defined by the RRA as a particular type of direct discrimination. Providing separate washing facilities for white and Asian employees, even if the facilities are of the same standard, might be an example of segregation on racial grounds. Similarly, only employing ethnic minorities in 'back room' roles where they have no contact with the public but allowing others a full range of roles and duties might be an example of segregation on racial grounds.

Indirect race discrimination

Indirect discrimination aims to challenge practices and procedures which on their face apply in the same way to everyone, but which in practice have different, unfair effects on certain groups.

Indirect race discrimination is defined in the employment context and several others as being the application of a specific provision, criterion or practice, which places a racial group at a disadvantage, in a way that cannot be justified. You can only bring a complaint if you suffer the disadvantage yourself. The following are examples of indirect race discrimination:

⇨ A policy that requires all employees to be clean-shaven, as this would put Sikhs in general at a disadvantage.

⇨ A practice of excluding job applicants who live in a certain area of a city where that area is occupied by a higher proportion of ethnic minority people, as this would put ethnic minority candidates at a disadvantage.

Unlike direct discrimination, indirect discrimination can be justified. If the person doing the discrimination can show that the provision, criteria or practice is objectively justified on grounds other than race, then the discrimination will not be unlawful.

There is another, older, legal definition of indirect discrimination which refers to a 'condition or requirement' rather than a 'provision, criterion or practice'. Although the new definition applies to claims of discrimination in employment, education, services and certain public functions such as healthcare, the old definition will continue to apply to other sorts of discrimination, which makes the law in this area complex. Therefore, if you consider that you have been indirectly discriminated against you should consider seeking specialist help.

Victimisation

Victimisation occurs when one person treats you less favourably than he or she treats, or would treat, someone else in those particular circumstances because you have done any of the following 'protected acts':

⇨ Alleged that the discriminator or any other person has committed an act which (whether or not the allegation so states) would amount to a contravention of the RRA.

⇨ Brought proceedings against the discriminator or any other person under the RRA.

⇨ Given evidence or information in connection with proceedings brought by any person against the discriminator or any other person under the RRA.

⇨ Otherwise done anything under or by reference to the RRA in relation to the discriminator or any other person.

The same also applies if the discriminator knows that you intend to do any of those things or suspects that you have done, or intend to do, any of them.

If bringing a claim, it is not necessary for you to show that the alleged discriminator was consciously motivated by the fact that you had done a protected act.

Allegations of discrimination must be made in good faith in order to be protected by the victimisation provisions of the RRA. An example of a situation in which a claim of victimisation might arise is where an employee accuses his or her boss of discriminating against him or her on the grounds of race and as a result of the complaint is demoted or disciplined. Alternatively, if a white colleague suggests that a manager has treated a black employee unfairly and then finds him or herself ostracised or subject to unwarranted criticism from that manager or his employer, this too might amount to unlawful victimisation.

Racial harassment

Regulations introduced in 2003 amended the RRA to make it unlawful for an individual to harass you on racial grounds at work, in education, services and some other areas such as healthcare. Harassment is defined as unwanted conduct which has the purpose or effect of violating your dignity or creating an intimidating, hostile, degrading, humiliating or offensive environment for you, on grounds of race or ethnic or national origins. This should be a useful tool for those who have been subjected to repeated bullying at work, as it is a more straightforward definition than that of direct discrimination. It should, however, be noted that, for technical reasons, harassment is only unlawful if it is on grounds of race or ethnic or national origins and not nationality or colour.

⇨ The above information is reprinted with kind permission from Your Rights. Visit www.yourrights. org.uk for more information.

© *Liberty*

Institutions must catch up with public on race issues

British institutions have not kept up with a public sea-change on attitudes to race and discrimination following Stephen Lawrence's murder, according to Trevor Phillips, Chair of the Commission

In a major speech today to mark the tenth anniversary of the Stephen Lawrence Inquiry, Mr Phillips argues the British people no longer tolerate racism in the way they did ten years ago. Yet our public institutions still have some way to go in ensuring that they treat everybody fairly and root out discrimination.

However, he also argues that using the term 'institutional racism' is no longer useful, as it has become cloaked in misunderstanding and creates defensive attitudes which could block reform.

'If we are considering the attitudes of the majority to the minority, today Britain is by far – and I mean by far – the best place in Europe to live if you are not white,' Mr Phillips says. 'The Nineties became the turning point when most people in Britain generally became comfortable with the idea of a black or Asian boss or spouse. And the trend is clear: the younger you are, the less prejudiced you are.'

'15 years on from that dark night in Eltham, we are a society more comfortable with diversity than ever before.'

The Commission today releases new research showing a new and growing diversity among the young. Almost 20 per cent of children under the age of 16 are from an ethnic minority and nearly ten per cent of children live in a family with a multiple white, black or Asian heritage. This growing diversity is one of the most fundamental changes we will see for over a decade, Mr Phillips argues.

But while the British public's view on race and diversity has changed so much since 1999, British institutions have failed to keep pace, he says.

Ethnic minorities are twice as likely to be poor as white people. Young black and Asian men are several times

as likely to be stopped and searched in the street by the police, and an African Caribbean young man is at least as likely to go to jail as he is to university.

British people no longer tolerate racism in the way they did ten years ago

---

Mr Phillips says that 'institutional racism' as it was described in the Stephen Lawrence Inquiry has not been obliterated from our public bodies. The unwitting prejudice, ignorance, thoughtlessness and racist stereotyping that Macpherson found has not disappeared.

However, he argues that while there is still an institutional bias against certain sections of the population, including ethnic minorities, the use of the term 'institutional racism' is no longer effective or appropriate.

'The phrase 'institutional racism' has become cloaked in misunderstanding,'

Mr Phillips says. 'It should be a way of helping us to understand the blockages in the system that turn organisations of decent, fair-minded people into opportunity deserts for women or ethnic minorities.'

'Yet it has never been read that way by most of those who needed to change. People came to think it meant that an organisation is permanently infected by racism from top to bottom; that somehow police officers become racists as soon as they don their uniforms – and that they can never change.'

'We need to stop re-running the same old argument as though nothing has changed. That is because we have actually succeeded in gaining much change... and because we face a new challenge that needs new methods and new remedies.'

Mr Phillips also argues that the phrase 'institutional racism' no longer captures the whole set of issues that we face as a modern country. People can be treated unfairly by public bodies, whether as employees or as members of the public, on a range of counts: their gender, sexual orientation, age, faith, disability and sexual identity.

'In fact, we still live in a Britain where the most important contributor to our life chances – educational success – is so strongly associated with our class and our race that we can predict which newborn babies will and will not succeed in life with some accuracy based just on their race and their postcode,' he says.

Mr Phillips also warns that the recession could have implications both for tolerance and the way people are treated by employers: 'We all know that the in the wake of the lean times can come resentment and division, all too often along the lines of race and faith. If this recession lasts more than months we know that there is a greater danger. It is that we start to turn the clock back on crucial advances that have been made in the years since Stephen Lawrence died.' He said that Britain had to ensure that

the recession did not start a 'counter-revolution' against the progress of the last 30 years.

Mr Phillps argues that the proposed Equality Bill provides an opportunity to address inequality in a way that chimes with the new mood amongst British people who are 'open, tolerant and fair-minded, yes; but impatient of bureaucracy and hostile to unnecessary, authoritarian interference in our everyday lives.'

Mr Phillips says the Equality Bill should simplify the thousands of pages of complex legislation and help local authorities and other public services improve. 'We need to see a dramatic reduction in the red tape involved in complying with equality law and stop the bureaucratic paper chase. If not, the danger is that we will create public services that are expert at superficial ticking of boxes but don't

actually change people's lives.'

And, he says, our legislators will have to change as well. 'We have a Parliament which itself is the outstanding example of racial, gender and disability exclusion... its lifeblood is white, straight and male. That has to change.'

'2009 could be the year that changes Britain,' Mr Phillips concludes: 'That would be the legacy that the Stephen Lawrence Inquiry deserves; and it would be the revolution we owe to Stephen Lawrence for the collective failure to protect his right to life.'
19 January 2009

⇨ The above information is reprinted with kind permission from the Equality and Human Rights Commission. Visit www.equalityhumanrights.com for more information.

© *Equality and Human Rights Commission*

Race equality in the UK

Why we still have a long way to go

The tenth anniversary of the MacPherson report was marked by the proclamation by deputy minister for women and equality Maria Eagle that great strides have been made in terms of race relations in the last decade.

The MacPherson report, initiated after the flawed police investigation into the murder of Stephen Lawrence by a gang of white, racist youths, was a defining moment in the history of race relations in Britain, because it acknowledged what we – visible minorities from black and Asian communities – already knew: that the police and many other public organisations are 'institutionally racist'.

MacPherson defined institutionalised racism as:

'The collective failure of an organisation to provide an appropriate and professional service to people because of their colour, culture or ethnic origin. It can be seen or detected in processes, attitudes and behaviour which amount to discrimination through unwitting prejudice, ignor-

ance, thoughtlessness, and racist stereotyping which disadvantage minority ethnic people.'

But just how far have we actually travelled on the road to equality in the UK? What has actually changed? Unfortunately, the answer is very little, if you look beyond the rhetoric to examine the facts and figures.

For starters, whilst the Metropolitan Police are making all sorts of proclamations of their own, claiming that the term 'institutionally racist' is no longer an applicable or 'helpful' phrase to describe the Capital's police force, this view is contradicted by the facts and by the testimonies of black and Asian officers.

Figures for 1997/8 showed that black people were five times more likely to be stopped and searched by the police than Whites. Stop and search figures for London between January and March 2007 showed that a black person is four times more likely to be stopped and searched than a white person and three times more likely to be arrested.

Figures released in February reveal

that in Suffolk, if you're black you're seven times more likely to be stopped and searched than a white person. Little progress there then. But such data should not be examined in isolation, but in conjunction with other statistics to create a clearer picture of the cumulative effects of racism.

For example, the fact that the black British community accounts for 15 per cent of the records stored on the national DNA database, even though we account for only two per cent of the UK population, alongside the disproportionate use of stop and search, point to the continued criminalisation of the black community.

But it's not just the black British public who suffer at the hands of an institutionally racist police force, but black police officers too. Who could forget the ordeal of former assistant police commissioner Tarique Ghaffur last year and his allegations of racism against Sir Ian Blair and other senior officers?

Ghaffur's claims came as the Metropolitan Black Police Association accused the Met of conducting a witch hunt against black officers and at the same time that Kent Chief Constable Mike Fuller revealed that black officers have to work twice as hard as their white colleagues to succeed, confiding that white officers tried repeatedly to stop him from being promoted.

The fact that Ghaffur was forced to back down from his claims of institutional racism is not in itself a vindication of Sir Ian Blair or the Met police, but rather evidence of its power to subdue those who seek to challenge it.

But the series of race rows that embarrassed the Met last year are compounded by fresh claims of racism and 'a culture of apartheid' at Belgravia station, where black officers were threatened with violence by their white colleagues and a Muslim officer was 'framed', according to allegations made at an employment tribunal.

The question is, does legislation bring about real change or merely create the appearance that racism and discrimination are being tackled, to appease those who believe in and fight for equality? If you believe that the latter is true then the forthcoming Equality Bill will do little to deliver substantive improvements.

Legislation may force individuals and corporations to change their modus operandi from overt discrimination to more subtle practices that are harder to detect and therefore harder to eradicate. This does not mean that legislation has not been effective and should not be used to tackle discrimination.

But it must be recognised that racial equality can only be achieved when attitudes in society change. You cannot change hearts and minds through legislation alone, and attitudes will not change voluntarily whilst ignorance and indifference prevail.

The cure for ignorance is education. But there is a dire absence of, as well as resistance to, education about race and its precursors – slavery, colonialism and imperialism. The government seems to think that denying that institutional racism exists in most of its public institutions and passing more legislation will make the problem go away.

But, as we've seen over the last ten years, denying a problem exists is not likely to yield much success in solving it. That's why in terms of race equality in the UK, we still have a long way to go.
12 January 2009

⇨ The above information is reprinted with kind permission from Colourful. Visit www.iamcolourful.com for more information.
© Colourful

Racism

Information from ChildLine

What is racism?
Racism is treating someone differently or unfairly simply because they belong to a different race or culture. People can also experience prejudice because of their religion or nationality.

It is illegal to treat people differently or unfairly because of their race and no one has the right to make you feel bad or abuse you.

What kinds of things do people do if they are being racist?
Racism takes many different forms. These can include:
⇨ Personal attacks of any kind, including violence.
⇨ Written or verbal threats or insults.
⇨ Damage to property, including graffiti.

Why are people racist?
Unfortunately, racism can exist in all races and cultures. Racists feel threatened by anyone who is from a different race or culture.

Our views and beliefs develop as we grow up. If a child or young person grows up within a racist family, or has friends who are racist, they may believe that racism is normal and acceptable. Prejudice of any kind is often based on ignorance and fear of anything unfamiliar.

I'm being bullied because of my race, what can I do?
If you experience racism of any kind it can make you feel lonely and sad. It might seem easier to avoid situations where the racist abuse might happen, such as not going to school, or staying at home all the time. This won't help it go away, and will make you feel worse.

Some things that you can do to help stop racial abuse include:
⇨ Accept that it's not your fault – you may feel less confident if you're having a hard time, but the thing you have to remember is that you are not the one to have caused the problem.
⇨ Tell someone what's happening to you, maybe a friend or someone at school like a teacher. Alternatively you can always call us to talk about what's happening.
⇨ Keep some evidence of what's happening (a diary of events, for example). This might be useful to show others that you need help.
⇨ Try and keep yourself safe. For example, you could walk home with someone you know rather than on your own.
⇨ Never give up! You might not be able to tackle racism by yourself. Seek out support and accept help where you can.

If you are worried about racism or are being bullied or abused because of your race, you can call ChildLine to talk about the problem at any time. You can also call us if one of your friends is suffering from racial abuse.

⇨ The above information is reprinted with kind permission from the NSPCC. Visit www.childline.org.uk for more information.

Hate crime

Information from the Home Office

Hatred is a strong term that goes beyond simply causing offence or hostility. Hate crime is any criminal offence committed against a person or property that is motivated by an offender's hatred of someone because of their:

⇨ race, colour, ethnic origin, nationality or national origins;
⇨ religion;
⇨ gender or gender identity;
⇨ sexual orientation;
⇨ disability.

Hate crime can take many forms including:

⇨ physical attacks – such as physical assault, damage to property, offensive graffiti, neighbour disputes and arson;
⇨ threat of attack – including offensive letters, abusive or obscene telephone calls, groups hanging around to intimidate and unfounded, malicious complaints;
⇨ verbal abuse or insults – offensive leaflets and posters, abusive gestures, dumping of rubbish outside homes or through letterboxes, and bullying at school or in the workplace.

Our definition of a hate crime:

Any incident which constitutes a criminal offence, which is perceived by the victim or any other person as being motivated by prejudice or hate.

Facts and figures

In 2007-08:

⇨ Police recorded 4,823 racially or religiously motivated crimes in which somebody was injured, 4,320 crimes without injury, and 26,495 cases of harassment.
⇨ There were also 4,005 cases of criminal damage related to hate crimes.
⇨ The typical hate offender is a young white male (most homophobic offenders are aged 16-20, and most race hate offenders under 30).
⇨ The majority of hate crimes happen near to the victim's home while they are going about their daily business, and an offence is most likely to be committed between 3pm and midnight.
⇨ Most hate criminals live in the same neighbourhood as their victims.

(*Source: Crime in England and Wales 2007-08*)

What we're doing about hate crime

We are working towards:

⇨ increasing confidence in the criminal justice system and in other agencies that deal with hate crime;
⇨ increasing the proportion of victims or witnesses of hate crime who come forward to report what they've seen;
⇨ increasing the proportion of hate crimes brought to justice;
⇨ improving local responses to hate crime, particularly in areas that have disproportionate numbers of cases.

We are working with other government departments, the police, and community groups to review our policies on hate crime, and will be launching more initiatives and measures related to this issue in the coming years.

The law

⇨ The Crime and Disorder Act 1998 created a number of new racially and religiously aggravated offences;
⇨ The Criminal Justice Act 2003 introduced tougher sentences for offences motivated by hatred of the victim's sexual orientation (this must now be taken into account by the sentencing court as an aggravating factor, in addition to race or religious hate motivation).

The Racial and Religious Hatred Act

This law, which came into effect in 2007, makes it a criminal offence to use threatening words or behaviour with the intention of stirring up hatred against any group of people because of their religious beliefs or their lack of religious beliefs.

What you can do about hate crime

If offenders are going to be punished, hate crimes must first be reported to the police.

If you're uncomfortable about going directly to the police, you can report hate crime anonymously through one of the following organisations, which will also be able to provide you with practical and emotional support:

⇨ Victim Support
www.victimsupport.org.uk
⇨ Equality and Human Rights Commission
www.equalityhumanrights.com
⇨ Citizens Advice Bureau
www.citizensadvice.org.uk
⇨ Galop – London's lesbian, gay, bisexual and transgender community safety charity
www.galop.org.uk

⇨ The above information is reprinted with kind permission from the Home Office. Visit www.homeoffice.gov.uk for more information.

© *Crown copyright*

Press reporting of violent crime fuels racism

Information from the Runnymede Trust

A new report from the Runnymede Trust has found that the print media's reporting of violent crime stirs racist tension. The researchers analysed reporting of violent crime in 2007 and identified different approaches to reporting of crime dependent on whether the victim or perpetrator are black or white. The authors argue that these approaches serve to influence public opinion and policy, and contribute to the reinforcement of racist stereotypes.

The deaths of black victims are of less concern to the print media than those of white victims

The tragic and disturbing patterns of violence between young people are a legitimate cause for concern and for media coverage. Too many young people are victims or perpetrators of violent crime in our towns and cities. Yet an analysis of the reporting of violent crime for two months of 2007 shows that the deaths of black victims are of less concern to the print media than those of white victims. When Metropolitan Police Commissioner Ian Blair pointed this fact out in January 2006 he was accused of 'crass insensitivity'.

Further, the report shows that the way in which violent crime is reported when the perpetrator or victim is from a minority ethnic background reinforces stereotypes:

⇨ Gang, gun and knife violence is regularly identified as 'cultural' and then attached to particular ethnic groups. The effect is that entire 'communities' are criminalised on the basis of their 'cultures'.

RUNNYMEDE

⇨ While it may be true that certain groups are responsible for a disproportionate amount of certain types of crimes, it does not logically follow that most members of those groups are involved in offending behaviour. However, this logical leap is often made.

⇨ Anecdotal evidence is too often treated as conclusive proof. For example, an inconclusive and brief Metropolitan Police report on the London gang profile was employed as evidence that the majority of young refugees are committing violence on the streets of Britain.

⇨ The media's reporting of teen-on-teen crime has been influential in defining the direction of crime policy in 2007. However, policies based on the assumption that black 'culture' creates crime, or

that 'black crime' is qualitatively different from 'white crime', are unlikely to be effective. Indeed, they may fuel racist responses and hold back effective work to tackle the scourge of violent crime in our neighbourhoods.

Michelynn Laflèche, Director of Runnymede at the time, said:

'The press is in a key position to provide information about people, places and events of which individuals and groups may have little first-hand experience. Needless to say, this power can be used to promote understanding and open-mindedness, or conversely, feed into vulgar prejudice. Therefore, it is alarming to think that while the language used in the press may have changed in the last 30 years, many assumptions linking minority ethnic groups to violent crime remain intact.'
18 April 2008

⇨ The above information is reprinted with kind permission from the Runnymede Trust. Visit www.runnymedetrust.org for more.
© *Runnymede Trust*

Perceptions of organisational discrimination

Proportions of people from minority ethnic groups who feel they would be treated worse than other races by public service organisations, 2001 and April-September 2007

Organisation	2001	April-September 2007
Any of the eight organisations	38%	34%
Any of the five CJS (criminal justice system) organisations	33%	28%
Local school	7%	6%
Local GP	4%	4%
Housing	13%	11%
Probation service	11%	10%
Crown Prosecution Service	14%	11%
Courts	14%	11%
Prison Service	21%	14%
Police	27%	22%

Source: 'Race, Cohesion and Faiths Statistical Release 2, Citizenship Survey April-September 2007, England & Wales', Dept. for Communities and Local Government. Crown copyright.

Say what you like, we have to get past this 'humour'

By Joyce McMillan

When I was a child growing up in the 1950s, every self-respecting infant in our neck of the woods possessed both a teddy bear and a golliwog.

The origins of both toys, and of their names, were largely obscure to us. Teddy was said to have something to do with the portly figure of King Edward VII, and Golly – well, there were no black children round our way, so I suppose we just thought of him as an imaginary figure, like those strange-looking characters from Disney cartoons who inhabit the toy counters today.

But that was then, and this is now. Back then, black people were still being systematically denied access to housing and employment in this country purely on the grounds of their colour. Back then, as President Barack Obama pointed out in his inaugural address, his own father would have struggled to be served in many restaurants and diners in Washington.

Back then, we were at the tail-end of a whole aeon of history – at least 2,000 years – in which white people of European origin, with their economic and political systems, had come to dominate the entire globe – for their own gain – and had come to believe, by and large, that they did so because of their natural superiority to other races.

And it is against this background, it seems to me, that we should discuss this week's almighty media hoo-ha over the case of Carol Thatcher, who – in a post-show drinks session at the BBC's *The One Show* – is said to have repeatedly referred to a French tennis player of African background as looking like a golliwog, despite protests from those present. It's possible to argue, of course, about whether the BBC has over-reacted in completely sacking Carol Thatcher from the show – a stern public reprimand might have been sufficient.

But what is clear is that the row has done Ms Thatcher no harm at all with the rest of the media, to whom the story has come as a godsend, in a week otherwise dominated by gathering economic gloom.

On one hand, it offers the commercial media yet another chance to continue their any-excuse rough-housing of the BBC. On the other hand, it offers a classic opportunity to claim mass public outrage over 'political correctness gone mad'; although in truth only 2,000 people – a tiny 100th of one per cent of the BBC's weekly audience in Britain – actually bothered to register a complaint about Ms Thatcher's departure.

And somewhere beyond all the hidden agendas, there also lies a serious debate about the limits of free speech in a society trying to move on from a racist and colonialist past; although it's a debate in which some thoroughly depressing views have been expressed this week, by those who seek to defend Carol Thatcher's remarks. For, as London papers with genuinely diverse teams of senior writers are now beginning to point out, black people in Britain almost universally find the idea and the image of the 'golliwog' offensive.

It is easy enough to see why: the toy represents a grotesque caricature of the 'Negro' as a comic figure – a little less than human, a little more than scary. And for any white person with any manners, and any sense of history, that black objection should be enough to rule the word, and the thing itself, out of polite company in Britain for good; not banned by law, of course, but simply excluded by decent choice, and by common courtesy towards the feelings of people who are, or should be, fully included in our national conversation.

'Oh, but this happens to every ethnic group,' comes the loud riposte from conservative middle Britain. 'Look, only the other day in Australia, Jeremy Clarkson called the Prime Minister "a one-eyed Scottish idiot". You just have to laugh it off. And why is it unacceptable to mock Muslims, but somehow OK to send up Christian beliefs? It's political correctness gone mad!'

But to those who make that most feeble of arguments, and ask that most disingenuous of rhetorical questions, I can only say that they should read some history, wake up to reality, and try to grasp what it has meant to be black or Asian on the face of this planet in recent times.

To poke fun at Gordon Brown is obviously to do what good comedy should do, in poking fun at one of the most powerful men on earth, and at a member of an ethnic or cultural group

SLAVERY

DISPOSSESSION

WE DON'T SERVE BLACKS!

I AM A MAN

JUSTICE FOR ALL

SECOND CLASS CITIZENS

– the Lowland Scots – who have played a hugely influential role in forming the world in which we live, and in profiting from its development.

But for a white person to poke fun at a black man for his hair, his skin colour, his looks, his faith – that is to raise historical spectres of a completely different order. That is to restate, and to seek social acceptance for, the lethal assumption of racial superiority – 'we' are normal, 'they' look funny – that was bred in our bones, until less than a generation ago, and which each of us now has to observe in ourselves, and fight to overcome, every day of our lives, if we are interested in continuing our journey towards a world in which human beings are finally valued and respected for themselves, in all their diversity.

And although, in a free country, we may say what we like without incurring the wrath of the law, we must also be prepared to take the professional consequences when we choose to insult a large part of our paying public, in a spasm of churlish nostalgia for a past we should be glad to leave behind, and in pursuit of the kind of barren and backward-looking joke that makes laughter die on the lips.

7 February 2009

© *The Scotsman*

Whatever happened to free speech?

Britain was once renowned around the world for defending people's right to speak out. Not any more, says Philip Johnston

The refusal to admit the oddball Dutch MP Geert Wilders to Britain yesterday marks a further retreat from this country's traditions of free speech. It stands in stark contrast to what happened exactly 20 years ago tomorrow, when Ayatollah Khomeini of Iran issued a *fatwa* calling for the death of Salman Rushdie for insulting the Prophet Mohammed in his book *The Satanic Verses*.

In retrospect, that was a turning point in the country's history of free speech, an event that appeared to demonstrate indomitability, yet turned out to be a defeat. An unambiguous stand was taken on Rushdie's behalf by the government of the day, which denounced the threat to his life and broke off diplomatic relations with Iran. Sir Geoffrey Howe, then foreign secretary, told the Commons: 'This action is taken in plain defence of the right within the law of freedom of speech and the right within the law of freedom of protest.'

Despite mass book burnings, protests around the world, including in Bolton and Bradford, and threats of violence, the work continued to be published and sold. How could it be otherwise? This was Britain, after all, the citadel of free speech. We would not be brow beaten into denying the rights of one of our citizens, or anyone else for that matter, from having their say, however controversial or offensive their opinion might be.

Sadly, the past two decades have seen a pusillanimous flight into cowering capitulation. We seem to have forgotten what free speech entails, how hard it was fought for and how important it is to defend. It is the value with which this country is most associated throughout the world. It is why Britain has been home, over the centuries, to so many political dissidents who would have been persecuted elsewhere, and why those who live in autocracies that brook no criticism tune into the BBC World Service.

They see this as a place able to accommodate opinions that are obviously crazy, offensive or even seditious, a country where a view can be held and expressed, provided – and this has always been true – that it does not foment violence.

Geert Wilders is an anti-Islamist who regards the Koran as inherently inflammatory and believes he is justified in saying so. He has made a 17-minute film, *Fitna* – an Arabic word meaning test of faith – setting out this thesis and was invited to show it at a private screening in the House of Lords. The film can be seen on the Internet, so there is no question of stopping its dissemination. It contains some unpleasant images of bomb explosions, of captured hostages facing death and of chanting mobs interlaced with passages from the Koran.

Wilders claims that these verses from the holy book of Islam are being used today to incite modern Muslims to behave violently and anti-democratically. You may think he is wrong to say this; you may agree with him; you might, like the lords who invited him to Britain, think it is something worthy of discussion, given the obvious problems caused around the world by radical Islamism and the violence perpetrated in the name of the religion. It is hard, in a free country, to understand why it is a view that must be suppressed.

What, then, possessed the Home Office to ban Wilders – an unprecedented action against a democratically-elected politician from a European state, who is entitled to free movement within the EU? By any measure, it was an extraordinary decision; yet it was not even raised in parliament, the supposed guardian of our freedoms, though some MPs have commented on the ban, largely to support it.

Were Wilders a terrorist preaching violence against particular groups, it could be understood on public order grounds. The order issued by

Jacqui Smith, the Home Secretary, read: 'The Secretary of State is of the view that your presence in the UK would pose a genuine, present and sufficiently serious threat to one of the fundamental interests of society. The Secretary of State is satisfied that your statements about Muslims and their beliefs, as expressed in your film *Fitna* and elsewhere, would threaten community harmony and therefore public security in the UK.'

Free speech is about understanding that some people hold a different view from you, whether you like it or not

---

Yet what possible threat to public security is posed by a Dutch MP showing a film, in private, to a smattering of peers on a Thursday afternoon in February? Of itself, the film does not call for violence against Muslims; indeed, it suggests that Islam is a cause of violence, a view with which you are entitled to agree or feel strongly about, but not to prohibit.

The reason for the ban appears to have been the possibility of protests by some Muslim organisations against Wilders's visit. In other words, his freedom to express a view and the liberty of peers to hear it in an institution supposedly devoted to free speech, were set aside in the face of intimidation – the opposite of what happened in the Rushdie case, even if that author was forced into hiding.

What is particularly insidious is the application of double standards. One of those most opposed to Wilders's visit is the Muslim peer Lord Ahmed, though he denies allegations that he warned parliamentary authorities that 10,000 demonstrators would take to the streets. Yet two years ago, Lord Ahmed invited Mahmoud Abu Rideh, a Palestinian previously detained on suspicion of fundraising for groups linked to al-Qaeda, to Westminster to meet him. When he was criticised for doing so, he said it was his parliamentary duty to hear Rideh's complaints. He does not

appear to see any contradiction with the position he now adopts against his fellow peers.

Had a foreign parliamentarian who disliked Christians and considered the Bible to be inflammatory planned a visit to Britain, does anyone imagine he would have been prevented from doing so? No, and neither should he have been. This must work for everyone.

The arrest and possible prosecution of Rowan Laxton, a Foreign Office diplomat, for railing at the Israeli invasion of Gaza from his exercise bike in the gym, is the latest example of an equally sinister development – the denunciation of opinions expressed in private, as with Carol Thatcher's 'golliwog' comments. Free speech is about understanding that some people hold a different view from you, whether you like it or not. When we start to alert the 'authorities' to thought crimes we really are one step away from the dystopian world that Orwell invented as a warning, not a prophecy.

The Government that has treated our liberties in such a cavalier way is having none of this, of course. David Miliband, the Foreign Secretary, said the film made by Wilders was 'full of hate' and therefore fell foul of British laws, though he admitted that he had not seen it and therefore could not judge. But, in any case, is he right? Is it against the law?

People have always been free under the criminal law to speak their minds, provided they did not, in doing so, incite others to commit violence or

infringe public order. Rabble-rousers trying to whip up the mob have never been the beneficiaries of this latitude: there is, in other words, a difference between license and liberty. However, it is necessary to demonstrate that the words complained of are likely to stir up hatred and public disorder, not merely to complain that they are unpleasant or objectionable to some. Imams have been allowed to continue preaching in mosques when it could be argued that they have overstepped this mark, as when they have called for the death of homosexuals or Jews.

Wilders is no advertisement for free speech. After all, he wants the Koran to be banned. But that is not the point. It is what this affair says about us, not him, that matters. Is Britain now adopting a position where people who support suicide bombers and *jihad* are able to make known their opinions without legal challenge, whereas those who oppose them cannot?

The very people who in 1989 were demanding the murder of Salman Rushdie for writing a book are today leading the charge against a Dutch MP for making a film. The fundamental difference is that 20 years ago, the government supported free speech; today, it has cravenly surrendered. It is simply not good enough to say that Wilders should not be heard because he might provoke a backlash from those who do not like him or his views. That is not upholding the law. That is appeasement.

12 February 2009

© *Telegraph Group Limited, London 2009*

Higher-tier test entry for Black Caribbean pupils

Information from the University of Warwick

Academically able Black Caribbean pupils are less likely to be entered for higher-tier maths and science tests than white children with the same achievement record, a University of Warwick study has found.

The finding, which has emerged from an analysis of test data collected on more than 15,000 14-year-olds, was presented to the 2008 annual conference of the British Educational Research Association in Edinburgh.

For every three white pupils entered for the higher tiers only two Black Caribbean pupils are entered

The Warwick University study found that Black Caribbean, Pakistani, Black African and Bangladeshi pupils were all under-represented in entry to the higher tiers of the maths and science tests that pupils in England take at the age of 14.

Further investigation established that prior attainment at age 11 could explain why Pakistani, Black African and Bangladeshi pupils were less likely to be entered by their schools for the higher-tier tests at 14. However, the different test-entry pattern for Black Caribbean and white children could not be attributed to performance at 11. Neither could it be explained by a range of other factors such as social class, gender, maternal education, entitlement to free meals, home ownership, single-parent households, and the higher truancy and exclusion rates among Black Caribbean pupils.

Dr Steve Strand, author of the study, says: 'After accounting for all measured factors the under-representation is specific to this one ethnic group and indicates that, all other things being equal, for every three white pupils entered for the higher tiers only two Black Caribbean pupils are entered.'

Tiering in national tests is presumed to be more efficient and to offer a more positive experience to pupils, since they are only tested on a range of items that are closely matched to their current level of performance, as judged by their teachers. However, the Warwick University study suggests that this assessment practice has unintended consequences.

Dr Strand notes that pupils who are not entered for the higher tiers are unable to achieve the highest test scores. But he does not argue that this contributes directly to Black Caribbean pupils' lower attainment and relatively poor progress in secondary school.

Instead, he says that it provides 'a window into teacher expectations and other in-school factors such as institutional racism' that may play a part in understanding the attainment gap for Black Caribbeans.

'Research suggests that teachers' judgments of students' academic potential can be distorted by factors such as perceptions of their behaviour,' says Dr Strand, who analysed data for 2004 gathered as part of the Longitudinal Study of Young People in England.

'Black Caribbean students may be disproportionately allocated to lower test tiers, not as a result of direct or conscious discrimination, but because teachers' judgments of their academic potential are distorted by perceptions of their behaviour.'

Dr Strand concludes that his study has implications for assessment policy in England. 'Proposals to replace tiered papers with single level tests, currently being piloted, will give even greater emphasis to teachers' judgments, since the tests will only be able to confirm the level teachers have entered pupils for, not indicate a higher level,' he says. 'These proposals may need to be reconsidered.'

8 September 2008

⇨ The above information is reprinted with kind permission from the University of Warwick. Visit www2.warwick.ac.uk for more information.

© *University of Warwick*

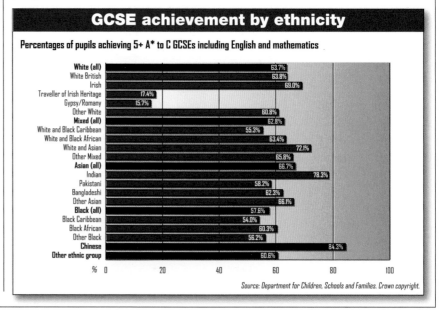

GCSE achievement by ethnicity

Percentages of pupils achieving 5+ A* to C GCSEs including English and mathematics

Ethnicity	Percentage
White (all)	63.7%
White British	63.8%
Irish	69.0%
Traveller of Irish Heritage	17.4%
Gypsy/Romany	15.7%
Other White	60.8%
Mixed (all)	62.8%
White and Black Caribbean	55.3%
White and Black African	63.4%
White and Asian	72.1%
Other Mixed	65.8%
Asian (all)	66.7%
Indian	78.3%
Pakistani	58.2%
Bangladeshi	62.3%
Other Asian	66.1%
Black (all)	57.6%
Black Caribbean	54.0%
Black African	60.3%
Other Black	56.2%
Chinese	84.3%
Other ethnic group	60.6%

Source: Department for Children, Schools and Families. Crown copyright.

White children have lower educational aspirations

Information from the University of Bristol

The proportion of white children with high hopes for their educational progress is much lower than for other ethnic groups in England. One of the key factors behind the difference is parents' aspirations for their children.

These are the findings of new research by Professor Simon Burgess and Dr Deborah Wilson of the Centre for Market and Public Organisation (CMPO) at the University. The study analysed data from a representative survey of over 14,000 14-year-olds in England.

Almost all pupils of Indian or Black African ethnicity plan to apply to university

The children were asked when they were aged 14 what they wanted to do at age 16: stay in school, take a job, seek an apprenticeship or something else. The research reveals substantial and significant differences in the percentages of pupils wanting to stay on at school across different ethnic groups:

⇨ Among girls, 85 per cent of white pupils want to stay on at age 16, compared with 94 per cent of ethnic Pakistani and Bangladeshi pupils, 95 per cent of ethnic Indian and Black Caribbean pupils and 99 per cent of Black African pupils.

⇨ The gap between groups is greater among boys: 73 per cent of white pupils want to stay at school, compared with 81 per cent of Black Caribbean pupils and over 90 per cent among the South Asian groups and Black Africans.

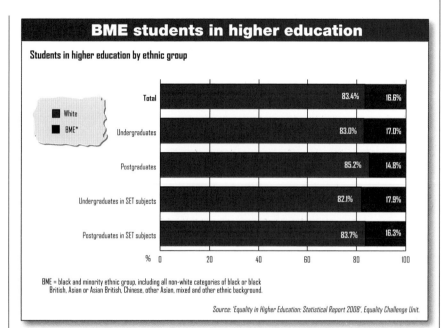

BME students in higher education

Students in higher education by ethnic group

■ White
■ BME*

	White	BME*
Total	83.4%	16.6%
Undergraduates	83.0%	17.0%
Postgraduates	85.2%	14.8%
Undergraduates in SET subjects	82.1%	17.9%
Postgraduates in SET subjects	83.7%	16.3%

% 0   20   40   60   80   100

BME = black and minority ethnic group, including all non-white categories of black or black British, Asian or Asian British, Chinese, other Asian, mixed and other ethnic background.

Source: 'Equality in Higher Education: Statistical Report 2008', Equality Challenge Unit.

⇨ The figures also reflect a strong gender difference for some groups, widest for white and Black Caribbean pupils, and zero for ethnic Indian pupils.

The survey also asked the 14-year-olds about their longer-term hopes of going to university and career aspirations. Again, there are large differences:

⇨ Almost all pupils of Indian or Black African ethnicity plan to apply to university.

⇨ About 15 per cent of Bangladeshi, Pakistani and Black Caribbean think it unlikely that they will apply.

⇨ 30 per cent of white pupils think it unlikely that they will apply.

⇨ There is little difference across groups in the importance of having a career at all, but big differences in the importance attached to getting ahead and getting promoted.

The research uncovers a number of reasons for the differences, including pupils' ability and academic self-image, family characteristics, school and neighbourhood. One of the most important factors is parents' aspirations for their children:

⇨ Among Indian, Pakistani, Bangladeshi, Black Caribbean and Black African families, over 90 per cent of parents want their child to stay on at school at age 16, compared with 77 per cent of white families.

16 December 2008

⇨ The above information is reprinted with kind permission from the University of Bristol. Visit www.bristol.ac.uk for more information.

© *University of Bristol*

Religion and nationality – the new 'race'?

Information from the Institute of Education

Educational performance tables comparing exam results of pupils from different ethnic groups are fuelling a new kind of racism, a leading academic has warned.

The tables, produced by the government, encourage schools to view some ethnic groups as natural high achievers – the 'model minorities' – and others as the 'failing minorities', always at the bottom, Professor Heidi Safia Mirza, from the Institute of Education, London, will argue in a lecture on 25 November.

'We have moved from biological notions of innate differences in the 19th century to religious, national and cultural notions of inborn differences now,' she will claim.

'For example, people say: "blacks are good at sport; Chinese are good at maths and make good food; Indians have good business sense".'

Professor Mirza will criticise 'superficial' attempts to teach pupils about different cultures for skimming over the real issue, which

Leading education and social research
Institute of Education
University of London

is entrenched racism. 'Bringing food, dressing up and listening to music are all good for sharing and learning about other cultures, but racism runs deeper and needs a more sustained and direct approach,' she will say.

'The pressures of educational policy (such as league tables) cause the sifting and sorting of pupils into tiers and streams by perceived ability. The patterns are often racialised, with black children locked into the lower streams.'

Pointing to the lack of anti-racist training for new teachers, she will cite statistics from the Training and Development Agency for Schools in 2008 showing that 70 per cent of newly qualified secondary teachers in England do not feel well equipped to teach pupils from different ethnicities.

'They may only get an hour-long class on diversity in their whole training,' she will say.

Despite this, research shows that minority ethnic teenagers are more likely to be in higher education than their white counterparts.

'They are driven by what I would call "educational urgency" – a desire to succeed against the odds,' explains Professor Mirza. However, she warns that this form of success may be even harder to achieve in future: 'With the scrapping of grants, increasing tuition fees and the realities of long-term debt, the sheer motivation to succeed is not enough if the structures and systems militate against you.'
25 November 2008

⇨ The above information is re-printed with kind permission from the Institute of Education, University of London. Visit www.ioe.ac.uk for more information.

© *Institute of Education*

Racial discrimination at work

Information from Directgov

It's unlawful for an employer to discriminate against you because of your race. You're protected against racial discrimination at all stages of employment. Find out about your rights and what to do if you feel you're being discriminated against.

What is racial discrimination?

The 1976 Race Relations Act makes it unlawful for an employer to discriminate against you on racial

grounds. Race includes:
⇨ colour;
⇨ nationality;
⇨ ethnic or national origins.

Under the Act, it doesn't matter if the discrimination is done on purpose or not. What counts is whether (as a result of an employer's actions) you're treated unfavourably because of your race.

The Race Relations Act protects all racial groups, regardless of their race,

colour, nationality, religious beliefs, national or ethnic origins.

The different kinds of racial discrimination at work

The laws against racial discrimination at work cover every part of employment. This includes recruitment, terms and conditions, pay and benefits, status, training, promotion and transfer opportunities, right through to redundancy and dismissal.

The law allows a job to be restricted to people of a particular racial or ethnic group where there is a 'genuine occupational requirement'. An example is where a black actor is needed for a film or television programme.

It's unlawful for an employer to discriminate against you because of your race

There are four main kinds of discrimination:

⇨ direct discrimination – deliberate discrimination (e.g. where a particular job is only open to people of a specific racial group);

⇨ indirect discrimination – working practices, provisions or criteria that disadvantage members of any group (like introducing a dress code without good reason, which might discriminate against some ethnic groups);

⇨ harassment – participating in, allowing or encouraging behaviour that offends someone or creates a hostile atmosphere (e.g. making racist jokes at work);

⇨ victimisation – treating someone less favourably because they've complained or been involved in a complaint about racial discrimination (e.g. taking disciplinary action against someone for complaining about discrimination against themselves or another person).

Employers who don't stop discrimination, harassment and bullying by their employees may be breaking the law.

What is 'positive action'?

Positive action is where an employer provides support or encouragement to a particular racial group. It is only allowed where a specific racial group is badly under-represented among those doing particular work or filling particular posts in an employer's workforce.

The employer is allowed to provide special training to members of the racial group. They can also encourage members of the racial group to apply to do the work or fill the posts (for example, by saying that applications from them will be particularly welcome).

This does not mean that employers can discriminate in favour of the members of the group when it comes to choosing people to do the work or fill the posts, that is unlawful discrimination.

Positive action is not the same as 'positive discrimination', which is where members of a particular racial group are treated more favourably. Positive discrimination is unlawful.

What to do if you have problems

If you're being discriminated against at work

If you feel that another employee or a member of management other than your immediate boss is discriminating against you because of your race, talk to your immediate boss and explain your concerns. Your employee representative (such as a trade union official) – if you have one – may also be able to help.

If your line manager or supervisor is discriminating against you, you should talk to their boss or to the company's HR department.

Be clear in your mind about what you see as discrimination, and if necessary give examples in writing. Many employers have an equal opportunities policy, and you should ask to see a copy of this.

You should also talk to your employer if you're told to act in a way that you think discriminates – for example if you're told to treat someone differently because of their race, colour, nationality, ethnicity or national origins.

If your employer doesn't want to help, you may need to make a complaint using your employer's grievance procedure. You shouldn't be victimised for complaining as this would count as discrimination.

If you're still unhappy, you can make a claim of race discrimination to an Employment Tribunal. You could get in touch with the Equality and Human Rights Commission or your local Racial Equality Council, if there is one, for advice.

If you feel you were not offered a job because of your race

You can take your case to an Employment Tribunal. You may wish to take advice before doing this.

Where to get help

The Advisory, Conciliation and Arbitration Service (Acas) offers free, confidential and impartial advice on all employment rights issues. You can call the Acas helpline on 08457 47 47 47 from 8.00 am to 6.00 pm Monday to Friday.

Your local Citizens Advice Bureau (CAB) can provide free and impartial advice. You can find your local CAB office in the phone book or online.

Seek legal advice from a Solicitor or Advice Agency on contract conditions.

If you are a member of a trade union, you can get help, advice and support from them.

⇨ The above information is reprinted with kind permission from Directgov. Visit www.direct.gov.uk for more information.

© *Crown copyright*

Race inequality increasing in the UK workforce

Information from Business in the Community

Barack Obama won the US presidential election with a message of hope, 'Yes, we can!' His election showed the American dream to be alive: an African American with a very un-American sounding name won the most high profile management job in the world. 'Could it happen here?' we asked. We might not wear our values so brazenly – there's no such thing as the British dream – but surely opportunity and hope are as plentiful in UK society? Race is no barrier to success in the UK? Most commentators concluded that it wasn't.

---

33 years since the passing of the landmark Race Relations Act there is still a colour bar to jobs in the UK

Depressingly, this seems a long way from the truth. Bluntly, without major and urgent policy intervention and action from businesses, the message to ethnic minorities in the UK is: 'No, you won't'. Ethnic minorities don't and, as the investigation Business in the Community's Race for Opportunity campaign has recently concluded shows, won't ever hold a representative share of jobs.

A wasted opportunity for employers

33 years since the passing of the landmark Race Relations Act there is still a colour bar to jobs in the UK. This must ring alarm bells with both employers and policymakers. It is not just that it hints at the possibility of institutional racism in corporate Britain – it is exactly 10 years since the Macpherson Report

made that devastating finding about the Metropolitan Police in the wake of the murder of Stephen Lawrence. It is also a wasted opportunity for employers.

With our economy in such an unhealthy state, the potential to regress further is very real. In previous recessions ethnic minorities have been disproportionately represented amongst those being made redundant. There is no evidence that employers have willfully discriminated against ethnic minorities when job cuts have had to be made, but we should be prepared for a worsening of the current situation.

Why have we made such depressingly poor progress on closing the gap in employment between ethnic minorities and Whites? Is racism so deep rooted in UK society? Probably not, but the UK does have a problem with the race issue because, unlike the United States, we have no comparable civil rights history. We're very comfortable with the idea that race equality is more of an American thing.

If ever we want to reflect the multicultural society in which we live, it will mean shattering the last glass ceiling and having an ethnic minority man or woman as Prime Minister and Chief Executives of FTSE 100 firms. And to achieve this UK society needs to recognise that it has a problem with race. In this respect, the United States is a much more progressive society than the UK.

To again borrow from Barack Obama's rhetoric, it is time for a change, not just on moral grounds but on commercial grounds. If no action is taken now then the problem will not just remain, it will get worse and become a more obvious lesion on society. That is hardly the face that the UK wants to present to the rest of the world.

The report and its recommendations

The report is based on new research carried out by Race for Opportunity who used data from the Office for National Statistics (ONS) in order

BAME in management positions

BAME* in management positions by industry 2000-2007

Industry sector	BAME share 2007 %	BAME share 2000 %	CAGR 200-07 %
Public admin, education & Health	33.2	25.7	15.9
Banking, finance & insurance	25.7	23.1	13.4
Distribution, retail & restaurants	20.0	23.2	9.4
Manufacturing	9.8	13.0	7.4
Transport & communications	6.1	8.4	6.7
Other services	2.8	4.3	5.3
Construction	2.3	2.3	6.3
TOTAL	100	100	11.9

* Black and minority ethnic people.

Source: Business in the Community, 'Race to the Top: The place of ethnic minority groups within the UK workforce', December 2008.

to analyse the changes in ethnic minority populations, both in terms of total numbers and in the number achieving management positions and particularly senior-level jobs. It then broke the data down by region, gender, ethnic group and occupation to give an overall picture of the successes – and obstacles – on the path to management. By going back to 2000 the report also reveals how much progress has been made over time and whether the rate of change has increased or slowed down.

To shatter the last glass ceiling, words are no longer enough. Action is needed now. The devastating picture painted by this report demonstrates the need for immediate and constructive action by government and positive intervention by employers. Each must make a co-ordinated contribution to ensure that their actions have maximum effect.

The Government must make race an issue in its employment agenda and campaigns, just as it has done for gender. Until it acknowledges the existence of race we will not achieve race equality. To achieve this it must:

⇨ promote positive action to speed up progress of ethnic minorities in a way that both gives clarity to employers and does not stoke up accusations of unfair treatment against the white population;
⇨ invest in targeted projects to promote the progression of Black and Minority Ethnic (BAME) people into leadership positions;
⇨ ensure that the achievements of working class whites and ethnic minorities are recognised across the curriculum; and
⇨ ensure that talented BAME people progress in the public sector; and in all walks of public life. Only by leading by example can government show the private sector what can be achieved. Employers can contribute by looking at their own individual employment and promotion policies. A sustained, long term commitment to the agenda and recognition that it will take lots of small steps by lots of people are required.

This should include:

⇨ setting public targets and monitoring and measuring progress in an accountable and visible way;
⇨ taking positive action such as organising workplace mentoring, supporting employee networks and establishing links with the community to provide positive role models; and
⇨ ensuring BAME workers can see clearly how they can progress within an organisation, ensuring the talent pipeline is representative of the workforce and community. There can be no more 'old school tie' or 'one of us'.

Source: by Sandra Kerr, National Director of the Race for Opportunity campaign, Business in the Community.
7 January 2009

⇨ The above information is reprinted with kind permission from Business in the Community. Visit www.bitc.org.uk for more information on this and other topics.

© *Business in the Community*

Equality Bill criticised by employers as unrealistic

Information from Personnel Today. By Louisa Peacock

Controversial plans to allow employers to discriminate in favour of hiring ethnic minority job candidates have been branded unrealistic by senior employment figures.

The long-awaited Equality Bill, expected to come into force in 2010, will allow businesses to favour recruiting under-represented groups to their workforce if there was a choice between two equally qualified individuals, one from a minority group and one from an over-represented group.

Employment lawyers warned the plans would cause confusion in the workplace as to what constituted discrimination and what was deemed 'positive action' – the legal method of encouraging black and minority ethnic (BME) candidates to apply for roles. This would discourage employers from using the new rules for fear of discrimination claims.

Speaking exclusively to Personnel Today, HR director Guy Pink, at drug and alcohol treatment agency Addaction, dismissed the plans as 'unrealistic', because no two interviewees can ever be considered equally qualified.

'The argument is that you'll get candidates that are equal at interview: but you'll never get two equal candidates at interview. It's unrealistic to think that. Ultimately you want the best people for the job.

'It changes the whole logic and professional approach to recruitment that has been drummed into us over the past 20 years: that you recruit the best candidate.

'If you start tinkering with that you undermine the approach to recruitment.'

Richard Kenyon, head of employment and pensions at Field Fisher Waterhouse, added the proposals could lull employers into hiring people based on their race or gender, rather than merit.

'The proposal actually means that someone who, through no fault of their own, happens to be in an over-represented group will potentially be treated less favourably simply by membership of that group,' he said.
1 December 2008

⇨ The above information is reprinted with kind permission from Personnel Today. Visit www.personneltoday.com for more information.

© *Reed Business Information*

New plans for achieving race equality in the UK

Information from the Department for Communities and Local Government

A wide-reaching consultation on improving opportunities for black, Asian and minority ethnic people was announced today by Communities Secretary Hazel Blears.

A new report demonstrates that the Government has made significant progress in tackling race inequality in everything from the job market and health services, to education, housing and criminal justice.

The Government has made significant progress in tackling race equality

The third and final report on the Government's race equality strategy, *Improving Opportunity, Strengthening Society*, shows that further progress depends on recognising that different ethnic groups are experiencing disadvantage in different ways. The Government is consulting on how best to move away from a 'one size fits all' approach to targeted help addressing the different needs of particular groups.

The consultation will also take account of the additional challenge posed by the economic downturn. Past evidence shows that black, Asian and minority ethnic groups, as well as disadvantaged white people, are hit harder than others because of the type of job they have or because they live in deprived areas.

Speaking at the Stephen Lawrence Conference in London to mark the tenth anniversary of the Macpherson report, Communities Secretary Hazel Blears said:

'Our research shows that the "one size fits all" approach to achieving race equality needs to change. Different ethnic groups are experiencing disadvantage in different ways and are not all in the same position.

'I don't believe there is any one "silver bullet" to solve these problems. If we are to make further progress, especially in light of new challenges such as the downturn, we need to identify what has and hasn't worked.

'It is clear there are some black, Asian and minority ethnic community organisations doing great work to challenge and overcome disadvantage, for example organisations like the Runnymede Trust and Operation Black Vote. This is why today I'm pleased to confirm that we are making £12 million available to national and regional strategic partners working across a range of public services to tackle disadvantage or barriers to reduce gaps in outcomes for black, Asian and minority ethnic people. This includes action to support women, young people and people with disabilities from those communities.'

Government is keen to hear a wide range of contributions and ideas – not just from community groups, but businesses, local authorities, and public service providers too because it's vital that we hear voices from around the country. Communities Secretary Hazel Blears and Cohesion Minister Sadiq Khan will be taking the debate across the country.

To kick-start the debate a discussion document, *Tackling race inequalities*, is also being published. It invites views on what the Government's future approach to promoting race equality should be, asking as well as rights, what responsibilities there are for people from all communities in Britain to others and themselves.

Communities Secretary Hazel Blears added:

'Equality is not just a minority concern. No-one should feel left out of the debate, because everyone has a role to play in making this country fairer and stronger. Equality not only has benefits for individuals but for society and the economy too.

'Thanks to Government action, there's been progress. There's also been a change in attitude to even casual racism. For the majority of people in the UK, making racist jokes is no longer seen as acceptable.

'The Government wants a new blueprint for race equality. Britain

must dismantle barriers and build on the talents of everyone to compete in the global economy, making this country fairer and stronger.'

Welcoming the new consultation, Rob Berkeley, Director of the Runnymede Trust, said:

'It is crucial that efforts to tackle racism, discrimination and inequality include strong leadership from Government. This consultation gives the opportunity to reflect on what has been achieved and to redouble our collective efforts to build a successful multi-ethnic Britain.'

'We've come a long way since the MacPherson report, including the Race Equality Duty which has fundamentally changed the way public bodies think about delivering their services'

Simon Woolley, Director of Operation Black Vote, added:

'The most effective way to tackle social and racial inequalities is to ensure individuals and community groups drive that agenda both in ideas and delivery. Government's role is to support and facilitate. All this requires a great deal of trust from all sides, particularly from central Government. Over the last few years we have been part of two initiatives: REACH, tackling the low attainment of black boys, and the last Communities and Local Government strategic partner's programme. Both have had elements of great success, precisely because of this unique partnership. If this approach can be built upon and replicated throughout the UK, our shared goals will be achieved sooner rather than later.'

Maria Eagle, Deputy Minister for Women and Equality, who today attended the Stephen Lawrence Conference in London to mark the tenth anniversary of the MacPherson report, said:

'We've come a long way since

the MacPherson report, including the Race Equality Duty which has fundamentally changed the way public bodies think about delivering their services.

'Our forthcoming Equality Bill will take this progress further: organisations will be able to take positive action to increase numbers of black and minority ethnic employees; transparency will be increased in the workplace; and laws will be strengthened to help tackle entrenched racial discrimination.

'But there's still a long way to go. We know diversity gives better informed decision making, so we are setting targets to increase diversity in Public Appointments, the Speaker's Conference is looking at the number of black and Asian MPs in the House of Commons, and we've set up a task-force to increase the number of black and Asian women in local democracy.'

Notes

1 The Government introduced the UK's first ever cross-Whitehall race equality strategy Improving Opportunity, Strengthening Society. The aim of the three-year strategy was to dismantle barriers in the public and private sector so people can rise as far as their talents can take them.

2 Copies of the report *Improving Opportunity, Strengthening Society* are available on: www.communities. gov.uk/communities/ racecohesion faith/

3 £6 million is available for up national and regional, third sector strategic partners across a range of public services. A further £6million will be available after the consultation finishes this May. Funding will be for financial years 2009/10 and 2010/11. Criteria for organisations interested in bidding for funding are available on: www.communities.gov.uk/ communities/racecohesionfaith/ grantsandfunding/

4 As part of developing a new race equality strategy, Government wants to have a robust and healthy debate with all communities about what the next steps should be. There will be a 12-week consultation asking what practical

Did you know that:

⇨ People from Indian backgrounds are more successful in education and employment than the rest of the population.

⇨ In 2005/06, the Pakistani population's rate of entry into higher education by age 19 was higher than that of the white population.

⇨ Black Caribbean pupils have seen greater-than-average improvements in GCSE Key Stage 2 and Key Stage 3 attainment.

⇨ In 2007, Chinese pupils had the highest achievement levels at GCSE (including English and Mathematics).

⇨ Black Caribbean men are still more than three times as likely to be unemployed as white men.

⇨ Women of Pakistan heritage have the highest economic inactivity rates at 65 per cent.

⇨ Among women, Black Caribbean women had the second highest employment rate and the third lowest economic inactivity rate.

⇨ Even if they're from better-off families, boys of Black African and Caribbean heritage, despite their positive attitude to school, do worse than white boys from a similar background.

⇨ Pakistani and Bangladeshi children are still twice as likely to grow up in poverty as white children.

measures should be taken to address disadvantages experienced by different groups. Further details on the new race equality consultation will be announced shortly: www.communities.gov. uk/publications/communities/ tacklingraceinequalities
24 February 2009

⇨ The above information is reprinted with kind permission from the Department for Communities and Local Government. Visit www. communities.gov.uk for more.

Is Black History Month still relevant?

Information from the National Youth Agency

Each year we religiously celebrate Black History Month and each year the perennial debate about the continued relevance of Black History Month in today's society resurfaces. In 2006, the Academy Award winning actor Morgan Freeman, in an interview with Mike Wallace on the American programme *60 minutes*, reignited the debate over whether Black History Month was still necessary. In the interview, Morgan Freeman called the observance of Black History Month 'ridiculous', igniting a firestorm of debate about its observance. Freeman asked a visibly shocked Wallace, 'Are you going to relegate my history to a month? I don't want a Black History Month. Black history is American history.'

Since Freeman's statement became public there have been numerous articles written by black intellectuals calling for the end of the celebration of Black History Month. The premise is that Black History Month is no longer necessary and by relegating its observance to a month it not only confines, but belittles and trivialises the historic contribution made by black people to society. Opinions are divided. There are those who, like Freeman, are of the view that black history should be incorporated into mainstream history, while others are equally clear on the value of Black History Month and its role in challenging 'imperial amnesia'.

Two students, Francis Joseph and Charlene Edwards, as part of their Black History Month project, collated a range of views for *Vibes and Voices* on the continued relevance of Black History Month in today's society:

'Black History Month (BHM) provides us with an opportunity to learn more about our history. As young people we only know the barebones of our history, BHM provides us with a wonderful opportunity to add flesh to the bones and make history come alive.'

'Black History Month is important to show erased history.'

'In an ideal world we would not need a BHM, but we do not live in an ideal world.'

'As long as we are not taught the truth about our history, as long as people fail to recognise and continue to ignore our contribution to history then there is a need for a BHM to celebrate our achievements of the past and to chart a route for the future.'

'BHM is very relevant in today's society because it provides an opportunity to glean a great deal of information historically ignored in mainstream education systems.'

'I think that we need BHM to mark the contribution and place of black people in British society. It is vital for us to celebrate our history.'

'BHM is designed to make a difference in the perceptions and attitudes of both Blacks and Whites. It offers a glimpse of the achievements of black culture.'

'We need BHM because we don't get an opportunity to sit side by side with the rest of history.'

'As long as British history is seen as white history we need to keep BHM.'

'As long as racism continues to exist in this society, as long as black children continue to face higher levels of exclusion from schools, are labelled as underachievers and are criminalised in the process we need a BHM to show the positive side of our black ancestry as positive contributors and makers of history.'

'Our history should be celebrated all year round, thereby eliminating the need for a designated month.'

'BHM helps us to understand the experiences of our ancestors as real, interesting and relevant.'

'BHM provides us as black people with an opportunity to gain a wider insight into our heritage, for reflection on the progress that we have made as a race and the road that we still have to travel.'

'It is disappointing that we have only a small time frame for insight and learning. That brings into question the true value that the wider society places on this annual event.'
Autumn 2008/Winter 2009

⇨ The above information is reprinted with kind permission from *Vibes and Voices*. Visit www.nya.org.uk for more information.
© *National Youth Agency*

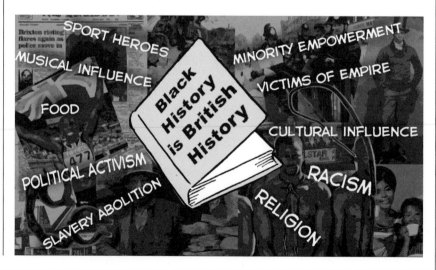

Gypsies and Travellers experience racism

Information from the University of Bristol

A new research review out today [18 March] shows that Gypsy and Traveller communities in Britain experience extensive inequalities, including pervasive racism and discrimination.

Some of the key findings of the report by Sarah Cemlyn from the University's School for Policy Studies, Margaret Greenfields from Buckinghamshire New University and the Friends, Families and Travellers organisation are that:

⇨ the lack of suitable secure accommodation underpins many of the inequalities that Gypsy and Traveller communities experience;

⇨ Gypsies and Travellers die earlier than the rest of the population;

⇨ Gypsies and Travellers experience worse health, yet are less likely to receive effective, continuous healthcare;

⇨ children's educational achievements are worse and declining (contrary to the national trend);

⇨ participation in secondary education is extremely low, with discrimination and abusive behaviour on the part of staff and students frequently cited as reasons for leaving education early;

⇨ employment rates are low, and poverty high;

⇨ there is an increasing problem of substance abuse among unemployed and disaffected young people;

⇨ there are high suicide rates among the communities;

⇨ children suffer psychological damage from repeated brutal evictions, tensions associated with insecure lifestyles, and hostility from the wider population;

⇨ Gypsies and Travellers who are forced to move into bricks-and-mortar housing can experience the worst housing conditions, combined with racist hostility from neighbours and isolation from their communities;

⇨ for some particularly excluded groups of young Gypsies and Travellers, there is a process of accelerated criminalisation, reflecting racism within the criminal justice system, and leading rapidly to custody;

⇨ within prisons, the perpetuation of discrimination, disadvantage and cultural dislocation can lead to acute distress and frequently suicide;

⇨ there is a lack of access to culturally appropriate support services for people in the most vulnerable situations, such as women experiencing domestic violence.

'Stereotyping and racism is pervasive and often overt'

According to Sarah Cemlyn, the report's lead author:

'This review reveals severe and far-reaching inequalities and discrimination affecting Gypsies and Travellers. Underpinning many of these is the lack of appropriate accommodation for between a fifth and a quarter of caravan-dwelling Gypsies and Travellers, resulting in lack of basic facilities of water and sanitation, lack of security, and frequent and sometimes brutal evictions.

'However the report goes well beyond this in reviewing inequalities across multiple policy areas including education, health, social care, employment, criminal justice and community cohesion. It found that stereotyping and racism is pervasive and often overt, frequently fuelled by misleading media reporting. Children are particularly vulnerable to racism from people in authority, members of the public and other children.'

Margaret Greenfields added that:

'The review explores a range of issues which have so far been overshadowed by the necessity of providing adequate accommodation for marginalised members of these minority communities. We have welcomed the opportunity afforded by the Equality and Human Rights Commission (EHRC) commissioning this review to move beyond this and consider not only the prejudice and inequalities experienced by Gypsies and Travellers, but also good practice, especially that developed by Gypsies and Travellers themselves despite being faced with almost overwhelming odds.'

The research team highlighted that the review contains detailed recommendations for each policy area investigated, while highlighting the urgency of providing sufficient sites, the necessity for service providers to fulfil race equality duties under the Race Relations (Amendment) Act 2000 in providing culturally appropriate services, and the importance of developing solutions in consultation with Gypsy, Traveller and Showman communities.

The report, entitled *Inequalities experienced by Gypsy and Traveller communities: a review*, by Sarah Cemlyn et al, which reviewed existing research across a wide range of policy areas, is published today by the EHRC.
18 March 2009

⇨ The above information is reprinted with kind permission from the University of Bristol. Visit www.bristol.ac.uk for more information.
© *University of Bristol*

Rise in anti-Jewish and anti-Muslim attitudes in Europe

Information from the Centre for Social Cohesion

Ethnocentric attitudes have been rising in Europe in the last two years, according to an international survey by the Pew Research Center, apparently reflecting concerns over immigration, globalisation and the current economic downturn.

The report, published on Wednesday, found increasing levels of anti-Semitism across Europe, with particularly strong negativity in Spain, Poland and Russia. The survey also revealed strong anti-Muslim views in those three countries, as well as in Germany and France.

'There is a clear relationship between anti-Jewish and anti-Muslim attitudes,' the report claimed. 'Publics that view Jews unfavourably also tend to see Muslims in a negative light.'

Older people, the less educated and those who considered themselves of the political right were more likely to be prejudiced.

By Hannah Stuart

Andrew Kohut, director of the Pew Research Center, believes immigration may be amongst the causes of the intolerance found. 'There may be some backlash toward minority groups going on in Europe as a consequence of the EU's expansion and globalisation,' he said.

Outside of Europe the report revealed pervasive worry about Islamic extremism. Majorities among many Muslim majority countries – including Indonesia, Pakistan, Tanzania and Lebanon – said they were concerned about the rise of Islamic extremism in the world today.

Similar numbers said they were concerned about Islamic extremism in their countries. Majorities in Turkey and Tanzania and nearly half of Indonesians also said there was a struggle in their country between groups who want to modernise the nation and Islamic fundamentalists.

Support for terrorism continued to drop, particularly in countries that have suffered from terror attacks. In Lebanon, the view that suicide bombing was always or sometimes justified more than halved, from 74 per cent in 2002 to 32 per cent. Significant minorities in Lebanon, Jordan and Nigeria, however, still endorse such tactics.
18 September 2008

⇨ The above information is reprinted with kind permission from the Centre for Social Cohesion. Visit www.socialcohesion.co.uk for more information.

© Centre for Social Cohesion

Rise in anti-Semitic attacks

British Jews' safety fears grow after Gaza invasion

Police patrols have been stepped up in Jewish neighbourhoods following the most intense period of anti-Semitic incidents to have been recorded in Britain in decades.

Some within Britain's 350,000-strong Jewish community accuse the government of not doing enough to condemn the increase in anti-Semitism

By Mark Townsend, Crime Correspondent

Safety fears are so acute that reports have emerged of members of Britain's Jewish community fleeing the UK with anti-Semitic incidents running at around seven a day this year.

Around 270 cases have been reported in 2009, according to figures compiled by the Community Security Trust (CST), the body that monitors anti-Jewish racism, with most blamed on anti-Israeli sentiment in reaction to hostilities in Gaza. Attacks recorded during the first Palestinian intifada of the late 1980s averaged 16 a month.

Scotland Yard is understood to have placed prominent Jewish communities on heightened alert, while the Association of Chief Police Officers' national community tension team is responding to intelligence by issuing weekly patrol directives to chief constables instructing them of threats to Jewish communities in their areas.

Incidents recorded by the CST include violent assaults in the street, hate emails and graffiti threatening 'jihad' against British Jews. One disturbing aspect involves the targeting of Jewish children. A

Birmingham school is investigating reports that 20 children chased a 12-year-old girl, its only Jewish pupil, chanting 'Kill all Jews' and 'Death to Jews'. In another incident a Jewish schoolgirl reported being bullied at a non-Jewish school because of the Gaza conflict.

CST spokesman Mark Gardner said the current fear of persecution was so profound that some members of the Jewish community were seeking to emigrate to countries where they felt more secure, such as Israel, the United States or Australia. 'I know two families, one of which has already moved and the other which is in the process of moving, who don't see the point of putting up with this,' he added.

This week the CST will publish its annual report on anti-Semitic incidents for 2008, which will reveal that around 550 were recorded in the UK last year, slightly less than the record of 594 in 2006, when Israel and Lebanon waged a brief but bloody war.

Veteran director and actor Steven Berkoff recently explained the anti-Israeli reaction over Gaza by saying: 'England is not a great lover of its Jews. Never has been.'

Some within Britain's 350,000-strong Jewish community accuse the government of not doing enough to condemn the increase in anti-Semitism. However, the Board of Deputies of British Jews said it had recently received a letter from the communities minister, Hazel Blears, stating that she was 'deeply concerned about the dramatic rise in anti-Semitic attacks in the UK'.

Mark Frazer, spokesman for the Board of Deputies, said: 'We are seeing an unprecedented level of attacks directed at the Jewish community, both physical and verbal. It is incumbent upon us all to isolate and marginalise those who would derail the legitimate political debate with an extremist and hateful ideology.' Recorded attacks have centred on the Jewish communities of Golders Green and Hampstead Garden Suburb in north London.
8 February 2009

© Guardian News and Media Limited 2009

Britain's forgotten race victims?

Information from the Runnymede Trust

In January 2009, the Runnymede Trust published a new study on the white working class and ethnic diversity in Britain. In response to Hazel Blears' call for white working class voices and grievances to be heard, leading thinkers on race and class consider the relationship between social class and race equality. They conclude that the white working class are discriminated against on a range of different fronts, but they are not discriminated against because they are white.

After a decade of being ignored, class inequality is making its way back onto the political agenda.

There are legitimate inequalities to be discussed and debated. Britain remains blighted by class division, and economic background is still the best predictor of life chances. Class is central to how people see their place in Britain today. Returning to the issue of class inequality and social mobility is therefore long overdue.

Various commentators have recently put forward the idea that white working class communities

 RUNNYMEDE

are losing out, while minority ethnic groups and immigrants are the winners at the direct expense of the white working class. The report disputes these claims and suggests ways of discussing class which can lead to greater solidarity rather than further division. It argues that the current way class is used puts it in opposition to efforts to promote race equality, rather than creating a means of pursuing increased equality for all.

Rob Berkeley, Director of Runnymede, said:

'There is an urgent need to ensure that a re-emergence of class onto the political agenda will not feed divisions, but promote equality for everyone. The way in which the debate has been framed so far hasn't been particularly constructive. The message from this publication is that it's possible to have a progressive debate on race and class in 21st-century Britain that can lead to better outcomes for all.'
22 January 2009

[The report] argues that the current way class is used puts it in opposition to efforts to promote race equality, rather than creating a means of pursuing increased equality for all

⇨ The above information is reprinted with kind permission from the Runnymede Trust. Visit www.runnymedetrust.org for more information.

© Runnymede Trust

Multiculturalism – a cause for celebration

Information from the National Assembly Against Racism

One society, many cultures

Racism, discrimination and poverty are the main barriers to integration, not cultural diversity. The alternative to multiculturalism is to follow countries such as France, Denmark and the Netherlands in a model of enforced assimilation, where minorities are told that their labour and taxes are welcome, but they should abandon their cultural heritage. These policies cause isolation and prevent social cohesion.

Celebrating and respecting the contribution of different cultures to British society dismantles many of the racist myths that exist

---

By contrast, multiculturalism assists the process of integration and counters racism. Of course, multiculturalism cannot eliminate racism automatically. Anti-discrimination laws need to be strengthened; strong messages for equality and against racism must be promoted by local and national government. NAAR, working with UNISON, has developed the One Society Many Cultures campaign to promote and celebrate multiculturalism and debunk the myths. The campaign has produced a range of materials that can be used. They can be found at www.naar.org.uk and relevant articles at www.respecttrust.org.uk. For workplace-related race equality issues, visit www.unison.co.uk

Britain – a nation born out of migration

Britain's diversity is the result of centuries of inward migration: Romans, Saxons, Jutes, Vikings, Normans, Dutch Protestants, French Huguenots, the Irish fleeing famine, Jews fleeing Nazi persecution, refugees from war, Empire Windrush and Commonwealth citizens and subsequent migration from Africa, Australia, New Zealand, the Balkans and Eastern Europe more recently.

These different peoples have brought with them their cultural traditions and heritage, successively building up the rich diversity that exists in Britain today.

What is multiculturalism?

Multiculturalism is the right of groups and individuals to pursue their own cultural choices, heritage and faiths while respecting the rights of others to do the same. The British approach stands in contrast to that of other countries which insist that people assimilate into one culture. That approach caused tensions in other parts of Europe.

Multiculturalism is of Britain's liberal tradition. John Stuart Mill, in his famous work *On Liberty*, said that 'the sole end for which mankind are warranted... In interfering with the liberty of action of any of their number, is self-protection.' Imposing a single cultural identity seeks to constrain individual choice.

Multiculturalism – a necessary part of the campaign against racism

Celebrating and respecting the contribution of different cultures to British society dismantles many of the racist myths that exist. For example, Notting Hill, the largest carnival outside the Caribbean and Latin America, was a response to a wave of racist attacks and violence in London in 1958.

In the 1970s, support for neo-Nazi groups was countered through carnivals of music and culture, bringing together black communities in a coalition with the organised labour movement and musicians.

The attacks on multiculturalism

Recent years have seen sustained attempts to undermine multicultural Britain, blaming it for many problems in our society. Multiculturalism is scapegoated as a barrier to integration, responsible for Muslim radicalisation. It is even held responsible for the attacks in London on 7 July 2005. Such myths have encouraged far right groups who are increasing their votes off the back of racist hostilities.

Society is becoming more integrated, not segregated

Claims that we live in increasingly segregated 'ghettos' are gaining favour. However, research from population statisticians demonstrate that the opposite is true. Segregation is decreasing. Data from the last census reveals a pattern of increased dispersal and greater integration.

Britain is now a more racially diverse and integrated society than at any time in its history. This diversity has significantly contributed to the country's economic and social development and continues to do so today.

Multiculturalism helps promote a safer, more united society

Despite campaigns in the tabloid press and hostile reports claiming multiculturalism threatens our security, the opposite is in fact the case.

Politicians and the police must work with all communities, the vast majority of whom oppose terrorism, to gain effective intelligence to prevent any future attacks.

Following the 2005 bombings, the loyalty of the entire Muslim community has been questioned. However, a MORI poll conducted in 2007 showed that Muslims overwhelmingly support western democracy. Multiculturalism unites society because every culture is respected equally and given a stake. Those who seek to divide society, including through the use of terror, oppose multiculturalism.

'Segregation is not increasing, it is decreasing – government and academic studies all show that each group is increasingly spread throughout Britain.'
Dr Ludi Simpson, Researcher in population trends

⇨ The above information is reprinted with kind permission from the National Assembly Against Racism. Visit www.naar.org.uk for more information.
© National Assembly Against Racism

Cultural identity

Bullying based on prejudice and difference

Living between two cultures – a 'British' way of life and the culture your parents or grandparents grew up with – can be a rich and fulfilling experience, but there can also be conflicts and challenges. When teaching our children about their heritage and the traditions we would like to see them continue, it can be difficult to balance these with the more 'British' traditions and ways of life that they are growing up with and embracing. Simple things like food through to language show just how complex this can be.

'I need more information on cultural issues, how to blend the two cultures, and still keep your origins.'
Living, studying and working in Britain obviously shapes some of our values, lifestyle choices and even beliefs. However, for second and third generation (whose parents or grandparents, respectively, were immigrants) black and minority ethnic (BME) people, there are countless other factors contributing to our belief systems and everyday way of life.

'Children from different backgrounds are bound to act differently due to religion, race, etc.'
Religion, race, traditions, clothes, language, food, film and music can hold great significance in a large majority of people's lives, but for people from a BME background, cultural identity can be made up of influences which are not part of the mainstream society they are living in and can often be misunderstood and misinterpreted. This can lead to curiosity from other children, who don't understand why your child is different to them. Curiosity is natural, but sometimes this means that instead of asking them about their culture, they may make an issue of the differences as if they are negative in some way and this can lead to bullying.

By continuing the practices and culture you enjoy and view as important, in your home, in the way you dress, the language you speak or the food you cook, you are giving your children the opportunity to share, participate in, and value different cultures. This can help give them

the support they need to then share these practices with their peers from different backgrounds, and the confidence to be proud of who they are.

⇨ The above information is reprinted with kind permission from Parentline Plus. Visit www.besomeonetotell.org.uk for more information.
© Parentline Plus

Society damaged by policies on multiculturalism

Society is being damaged by Labour's politically correct policy of multiculturalism and the fear of causing offence, according to Dominic Grieve

Mr Grieve, the shadow justice secretary, claims the regulation of private opinions and public debate have left people unable to say what they think is right or wrong.

He believes Britain is suffering an 'identity breakdown' after a decade in which the Government has destroyed respect for the country's history and culture.

And he warns that the failure to discuss multiculturalism by mainstream political groups has been exploited by the far-right British National Party, which is now taking council seats across the country.

His comments come a week after Hazel Blears, the Communities Secretary, said people must be free to discuss contentious issues without fear of 'over-reaction'.

But speaking at the Lord Smith of Clifton Lecture at Queen Mary, University of London, Mr Grieve said: 'In fact if she is serious, she is heralding a U-turn on 12 years of Labour policy.

'A decade of ranking people as members of neatly categorised ethnic, religious or social groups, rather than treating everyone as an individual in their own right.'

By Martin Beckford, Religious Affairs Correspondent

He highlighted the cases of Caroline Petrie, the nurse suspended for offering to pray for a patient, and Jennie Cain, the school receptionist whose five-year-old daughter was scolded for talking about Hell to another girl, as examples of 'disproportionate reactions' that damage 'the worthy cause of promoting harmony'.

Mr Grieve went on: 'At the other extreme, the lack of a credible response from the mainstream right to the current issues of multiculturalism has now left a gap, which is being filled by extremist voices. UKIP and the British National Party have taken advantage to suggest policies not based on a reasoned morality but which play on fear and encourage hatred.

'The zealous regulation of conduct, the imposition of state-defined orthodoxy on public and private conscience and the overburdening of law and regulation, have the consequence of undermining that confidence and are deterring participation and engagement.

'Increasing prescription is robbing us of our ability to decide ourselves what is right and wrong.

'Indeed, the reluctance to exercise reasonable judgment and to criticise or challenge negative cultural imports into our country, including discriminatory practises against women and corrupt political and electoral practises, is one of the most troubling consequences of a culture that wishes to avoid offence and accusations of racism.

'Multiculturalism was intended to create a more cohesive and friendlier society by facilitating bringing people together. But instead the laws and concepts underlying it seem to me to drive people apart, endangering our traditional sense of community based on common values.

'I am convinced that this approach has hindered more recent immigrants to this country developing a sense of belonging. Faced with a society that seems to be suffering an identity breakdown, should we be surprised that they find a common identity with their fellow countrymen hard to identify?'

4 March 2009

© Telegraph Group Limited, London 2009

Second generation

We talk to teenagers, brought up in Britain but whose parents came from a different country, about their cultural identity

A different generation

Second generation teens are those who were brought up and often born in a country different from their parents' home country. Their parents might have come here to work or to try a different or better way of life for their family.

If you're a second generation teenager, you may have been influenced both by the way your parents have brought you up and by the customs of the country in which you live.

So what's it like being part of two cultures?

Fiona is 15. She was born in Britain but her parents are from China. Fiona thinks being part of two cultures is a good thing: 'I can identify with two whole different sides of the world.'

Tejas is 16. His parents are of Indian descent. He feels being part of two cultures has helped him: 'You feel more confident as you can relate to more people. I also feel much smarter and wiser because of the greater range of knowledge of two cultures.'

If you're second generation your identity may be very British, but you will also have many influences from your parents' culture

---

Two worlds

There are many benefits to being part of two cultures, however alike or different they are from each other. You might speak another language, eat different food or even have visited another country!

Seeing where your parents were born can have a great effect on how you live your life. You may even learn to appreciate what you have.

Tejas certainly did when he went to visit family in India. 'Living in India is extremely difficult for people like me because the living conditions are not as good as they are in England. It is also much hotter.'

Two sides

Being part of two cultures can be confusing though. Which traditions do you follow and which ones can you relate to?

Tejas agrees, 'We sometimes have to reject parts of one culture to follow another culture and this can often leave negative scars on individuals.'

Traditions

Traditions and values are a strong part of identity. Eating a Sunday roast, understanding British jokes or even watching *Eastenders* can all be seen as typical British activities.

If you're second generation your identity may be very British, but you will also have many influences from your parents' culture. 'I don't do anything particularly British, but there are some Chinese ways of behaving that I don't do,' comments Fiona.

Tejas is also influenced by both cultures. 'I adapted to the British lifestyle including eating – fork in the left hand and knife in the right. I also have a strong link with British sport, music and food.'

Values

Often, parents of second generation children might not understand the way young people think, because they grew up in a different culture with different values.

'My parents have more traditional ambitions – finding a job that pays well rather than one that I enjoy, getting married,' adds Fiona.

Tejas agrees, 'My parents believe that all individuals should not turn their back on God.'

However, second generation teens might not always adopt the same values. 'I think most of it has had the opposite effect on me,' says Fiona.

Culture clash

Being part of two cultures doesn't mean you have to choose between them.

Tejas has advice for young people who may be experiencing a 'culture clash': 'Remember not to completely forget about one culture for another. We may not want to listen to other people's views on certain topics but we have to as this is an aspect in belonging to two or more cultures. Don't let people stop you from being willing to accept other cultures.'

Fiona agrees. 'Try to keep both cultures going, because they're both a part of you and you can't change that.'
29 July 2008

➪ The above information is reprinted with kind permission from Need2Know. Visit www.need2know.co.uk for more information.

The rise of mixed-race Britain

Information from the Institute for Social & Economic Research

A new report commissioned from ISER's Lucinda Platt shows there is a new and growing diversity among young people that makes the very concept of black and white harder and harder to define.

Ethnicity and Family: Relationships Within and Between Ethnic Groups, produced for the Equality and Human and Rights Commission, indicates that the percentage of young people from ethnic minority backgrounds is on the rise, as is the number of young people from families with mixed heritages. According to the report, if current trends continue, ethnic minorities and those from mixed race backgrounds will make up an increasingly large proportion of the population in the future.

⇨ 20 per cent of young people under the age of 16 are from an ethnic minority background, compared to 15 per cent of the total population.

⇨ Three per cent of children under 16 are mixed race, compared to five per cent of adults.

⇨ Nearly 10 per cent of children under 16 live in a family with heritages from more than one ethnic group.

⇨ The average age for someone of a mixed race background is significantly younger than their white counterparts – 16 for those from mixed white and Caribbean backgrounds and 18 for mixed white and Asian backgrounds – compared to an average age of 40 for white British people.

The report also looks at the rise of inter-ethnic relationships, which it notes have often been seen as indicative of the extent of openness in different societies and of the extent to which identities are adapting and changing over time. They are, according to the report, 'taken to be a thermometer of ethnic relations in particular societies'.

⇨ 48 per cent of Black Caribbean men are in mixed race relationships.

⇨ 34 per cent of Black Caribbean women are in mixed race relationships.

⇨ Overall, younger people from most ethnic backgrounds are more likely to be in mixed race relationships; 10 per cent of 16- to 29-year-olds, compared to eight per cent of 30- to 59-year-olds.

Lucinda Platt suggests that the decline in partnerships among people from the same ethnic background may reflect a general view that race itself does not provide as meaningful a basis when selecting a partner, compared to other things young people may have in common like education, friends, attitudes and beliefs.

A spokesperson for the Equality and Human Rights Commission said:

'Britain is changing in a remarkable way. One in five of our children are from an ethnic minority background and young people are six times more likely to be mixed race compared to adults. The old, polarising debate about black and white is changing and the next generation will not see race in the same way we see it.

'This is hugely positive and we can afford a moment to celebrate: Britain's diverse culture is becoming all the more fascinating and inter-connected. But we can't afford to be complacent, because we face other challenges. We need to be alert to tensions within communities that may be exacerbated by the economic downturn and remain vigilant against discrimination and divisiveness – particularly across boundaries of faith.'
19 January 2009

⇨ The above information is reprinted with kind permission from the Institute of Social & Economic Research. Visit www.iser.essex.ac.uk for more information.
© *Institute for Social & Economic Research*

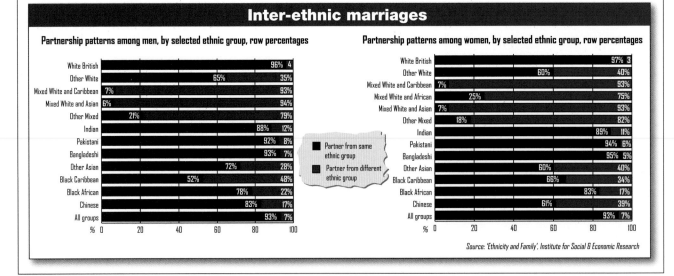

Inter-ethnic marriages

Partnership patterns among men, by selected ethnic group, row percentages

Ethnic group	Partner from same ethnic group	Partner from different ethnic group
White British	96%	4
Other White	65%	35%
Mixed White and Caribbean	7%	93%
Mixed White and Asian	6%	94%
Other Mixed	21%	79%
Indian	88%	12%
Pakistani	92%	8%
Bangladeshi	93%	7%
Other Asian	72%	28%
Black Caribbean	52%	48%
Black African	78%	22%
Chinese	83%	17%
All groups	93%	7%

Partnership patterns among women, by selected ethnic group, row percentages

Ethnic group	Partner from same ethnic group	Partner from different ethnic group
White British	97%	3
Other White	60%	40%
Mixed White and Caribbean	7%	93%
Mixed White and African	25%	75%
Mixed White and Asian	7%	93%
Other Mixed	18%	82%
Indian	89%	11%
Pakistani	94%	6%
Bangladeshi	95%	5%
Other Asian	60%	40%
Black Caribbean	66%	34%
Black African	83%	17%
Chinese	61%	39%
All groups	93%	7%

■ Partner from same ethnic group
■ Partner from different ethnic group

Source: 'Ethnicity and Family', Institute for Social & Economic Research

I have no doubt what colour I am

Let's get beyond the debate over whether 'mixed race' is synonymous with 'black'. It is

By Matthew Ryder

The question of whether someone who is mixed race is, in fact, 'black' has been the subject of much discussion since Barack Obama began to be taken seriously as a contender for president. For those, like myself, who are mixed race and had settled into our black identity a long time ago, the debate has been sometimes uncomfortable. While for some it was a moment for personal expression, for others the separation of 'mixed race' from 'black' is anathema.

It has been a debate that engaged this country more than the US. The proportion of mixed-race citizens, whose numbers famously include the Formula One racing driver Lewis Hamilton, is rising much faster here, and previously straightforward ethnic categories are being questioned by younger generations. With 63% of black Caribbean men born in the UK in mixed relationships, it is a trend that is set to continue.

It's useful to see how the next US president, a master of racial nuance, handles this issue. Obama celebrates, even jokes about, his own diverse background. The love of his white American family pours from his biography, alongside his deep connection to his Kenyan relatives. But there is no question that the world's most famous mixed-race man identifies himself as, among other things, a black man. His view, if you have travelled a similar path and reached the same conclusion, is a powerful affirmation.

Frequently in *Dreams From My Father*, Obama confidently refers to himself as a 'black man'. The book's account of a student named Joyce is strikingly familiar to any of us who have been in his situation. She shakes her head when the young Obama asks if she is coming to the Black Students' Association meeting. 'I'm not black, I'm multiracial,' she insists, and after relating her mixed origins she laments: 'Why should I have to choose between them?' It is black people, she says, not white, who are forcing an uncomfortable 'choice'. Obama is not persuaded. His empathetic criticism of her perspective is followed by his telling description of her as one of the 'black' students. How he would define her seems clear.

Why has he reached that position? For me, it is because he recognises the fundamental error of those who try to assert that 'mixed race' is separate from 'black'. They have misunderstood that the term 'black' has always included mixed-race and lighter-skinned people of African heritage. By its very definition, 'black' has not overlooked us, but embraced us.

Discussions about whether mixed-race people are 'black' often focus on racism's all-encompassing anti-pathy towards darker people; or the infamous 'one drop' rule that categorised all persons with some African blood as forever second class. We were all grouped together. A less racist society, the argument goes, would have recognised us as different, and it should do so now.

The problem with that well-meaning approach is that it is both inaccurate and reactionary. It was the most racist societies that highlighted such distinctions and, to our collective credit, we moved on. The American South proudly divided slaves into 'Negroes', 'mulattos', 'quadroons' and 'octoroons'. Apartheid South Africa, also differentiated between 'black' and 'coloured'. It is ironic when seemingly progressive commentators want to return to that position.

In deliberate contrast, 'black' did not make distinctions based on racial purity. There were two key reasons the term became ubiquitous in the 1960s. First, it was unifying. African-Americans, like Caribbeans, are a physically diverse, but culturally connected people. So to describe all those of African lineage with one label, spoke to that shared cultural heritage. Second, it was liberating. The phenomenon of everyone from 'Negroes' to 'quadroons' choosing to redefine themselves as 'black',

Black, me? No, I'm mixed race! I'm Irish, Caribbean, North African and British,

Like I said, Black!

regardless of skin tone or hair texture, consciously subverted a discredited history of oppression. The closeness to white ancestry was no longer the defining source of our identity. 'Black' was virtually revolutionary.

Once the genesis of the term is understood, the fallacy that 'mixed race' can or should be separated from 'black' is exposed. By definition, 'black' includes mixed race; to assert otherwise would mean changing what 'black' means. And, if so, are we supposed to invent a new term for a group of 'black' people who are racially 'pure'? No such divisive concept has been part of our culture in recent memory. Obama also describes himself as 'African-American'. Certainly, there are strong arguments that the term 'African' should now be embraced in preference to the term 'black', but that is a different debate. What it shows is how comfortably he wears the complexity of who he is. There

is nothing limiting about his version of blackness because it connects to a world view: 'Our trials and triumphs became at once unique and universal, black and more than black...'.

Barack Obama is mixed-race but is described by many as the first black president of the United States

Around the world, particularly in the UK, Obama has not merely raised the issue as to whether a person who is

mixed race can be black – if anything, he has settled it. The real beauty is his understanding that different identities can confidently coexist in the same person. His black identity is not hostile towards, or exclusive of, his white relatives. Perhaps, having resolved that issue, we can now begin to focus on the important business of what the first black president does, rather than continuing to agonise over what he is.

Social and ethnic demographics in the UK will shift dramatically in our lifetimes, as today's survey shows. If we embrace our own multiple identities and enjoy who we are, instead of arguing over what we are not, we can face the future with more confidence. That is why I, and many others like me, remain unapologetically and happily African, Caribbean, British, European, mixed race and, of course, black.

18 January 2009
© *Guardian News and Media Limited 2009*

Letters: Identity is about more than black or white

Letters to *The Guardian* responding to 'I have no doubt what colour I am'

Matthew Ryder ('I have no doubt what colour I am', Comment, last week) says that 'mixed race' and 'black' are the same. I am as proud of my Italian heritage as I am of my African one. How can either 'black' or 'mixed race' encompass my multiple identity? I describe myself as mixed race on equal opportunities forms and as mixed heritage to anyone who asks, but use black as a shorthand.

What is race anyway? Describing my identity as anything other than 'mixed heritage' feels reductive. I am African (Gabonese) and Italian; I am black and I am white; I am mixed race and mixed heritage. It depends on where I am, who's asking, when and how long I have to answer the question. Ultimately, I am a human being with an international family, who speaks four languages and feels at

home in Africa, Europe and America. With a bit of luck, I'm the future – and Enoch Powell's worst nightmare!
Elena Obiang Ondo, Ipswich

As a mixed-race person, I strongly disagree with Matthew Ryder's view. What he fails to understand is that many mixed-race people like me, who once ticked the 'Other' box, wanted both their black and white heritages to be acknowledged. To many mixed-race people, saying they are black above anything else is a denial of themselves and where they are from.

Ryder should be aware that not all mixed-race people do or should have the same view on their identity. People have no right to force a black identity and cultural expectations on mixed-race stars such as Lewis Hamilton (who's never spoken on how he identifies) and Tiger Woods.

We live in a multicultural society; isn't it about time mixed-race people were given the respect they deserve?
Ben Scarr, Barnet, Hertfordshire

My definition of blackness is having black African blood to any degree and being comfortable with it. The two do not, however, always go together and I suspect this to be the case in a good number of those who seek to re-categorise themselves as 'mixed race'.

As Mr Ryder pointed out, 'black' was defined a long time ago to embrace all those with a black African heritage. There is no such thing as a race by the name of 'mixed'. Rather than creating more and more divisions, we ought to be moving forward by working towards greater unity, ideally, a human race that stands as only one category of people.
Dorothy Onyekwe, Croydon, Surrey

Most people from the Caribbean are already of mixed race. It is also not true that an African heritage is the only significant one. Jamaica probably has the largest majority of people of mainly African origin, but Trinidad is divided between the descendants of African slaves and those of indentured labourers from the Indian subcontinent. Guyana has both these as well as many who stem from the indigenous Amerindian population. On the smaller islands, the picture is even more mixed.

There were also Whites whose forebears were sent there as convicts, before the slave trade really got going. Slave owners were not averse to having relations with their slaves and in later days there was never anything formal such as apartheid laws. The cultural results of all this are a fascinating study of a process which is clearly still going on.

Tamsin Heycock, London N5
25 January 2009

'Myths' threaten racial harmony

Race relations in Britain are under threat from a series of ill-informed myths, according to a new book by two of the country's leading experts on the topic

Using previously unpublished evidence, Professor Ludi Simpson and Dr Nissa Finney from the University of Manchester show how repeated falsehoods about immigration, integration and segregation are misguiding policy and promoting racial disharmony.

This is the basis of the authors' new book, *Sleepwalking to segregation? Challenging myths about race and migration*, published today by The Policy Press.

After years of investigation, the Manchester pair have found no evidence 'whatsoever' for the existence of race ghettos in the UK. In fact the opposite is true, with increasing ethnic mixing.

And claims by head of equalities watchdog the Equality and Human Rights Commission Trevor Phillips that Britain is 'sleepwalking' into racial and religious segregation are also dismissed in the book.

According to the academics' review of evidence, white flight is no greater than brown or black flight. And there is white movement into minority concentrations in Leicester, Bradford, Lambeth, Wolverhampton, Wyncombe, Manchester and Merton.

By linking social problems to segregated areas, they say, politicians have stigmatised the areas and their residents.

The authors also provide evidence that areas with large populations of Muslims do not act as a 'breeding ground' for terrorism.

'By propagating myths using bogus and alarmist interpretations of population change, individuals such as Trevor Phillips, Dr Michael Nazir-Ali, Bishop of Rochester and Sir Andrew Green, Chair of Migration Watch are inadvertently promoting racial segregation,' said Professor Simpson.

'Misunderstanding breeds mistrust and division between ethnic and religious groups. This book is about dispelling those myths. The truth is that Britain's so-called ghettos are diverse areas both ethnically and socially where no one ethnic group dominates.'

Dr Finney added: 'The only concentrations which resemble anything like ghettos are of white people. The average white person lives in an area which has more than 94% white people in it.

'British Pakistanis, for example, live in areas which on average have 26% Pakistani residents. In almost every city with a sizeable immigrant settlement area, children of immigrants have on balance moved away from those areas, not to them or between them. So it is wrong to argue there is retreat. Rather, we are witnessing dispersal.'
22 January 2009

⇨ The above information is reprinted with kind permission from the University of Manchester. Visit www.manchester.ac.uk for more information.

Rivers of blood survey

Information from Ipsos MORI

A survey conducted by Ipsos MORI from 11-13 April 2008 found that a quarter (25%) of British adults felt that local areas were losing their sense of Britishness because of immigration; a 13 percentage point increase from 2005. 24 per cent of those questioned believed that there was a 'great deal' of tension between people of different races and nationalities and 52 per cent said they believed there was a 'fair amount' of tension. Only four per cent thought there was no tension at all.

Topline results

⇨ Results are based on a nationally representative sample of 1,000 GB adults aged 18+ years.

⇨ Interviews were conducted by telephone using Random Digit Dialling.

---

24 per cent of those questioned believed that there was a 'great deal' of tension between people of different races and nationalities

---

⇨ Fieldwork was conducted on 11-13 April 2008.

⇨ Data are weighted by age, gender, social class, work status and Government Office Region to reflect the population profile.

⇨ When results do not add up to 100%, this may be due to computer rounding or multiple responses.

⇨ An asterisk (*) denotes a finding of less than 0.5% but greater than zero.

⇨ Base: All adults (aged 18+) unless otherwise stated.

18 April 2008

⇨ The above information is reprinted with kind permission from Ipsos MORI. Visit www.ipsos-mori.com for more information.

© *Ipsos MORI*

Public opinion on racial tension

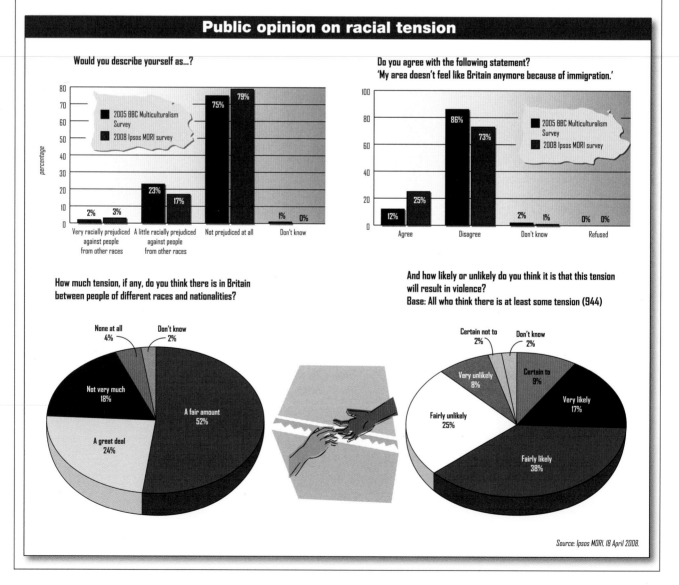

Would you describe yourself as...?

- 2005 BBC Multiculturalism Survey
- 2008 Ipsos MORI survey

Very racially prejudiced against people from other races: 2%, 3%
A little racially prejudiced against people from other races: 23%, 17%
Not prejudiced at all: 75%, 79%
Don't know: 1%, 0%

Do you agree with the following statement?
'My area doesn't feel like Britain anymore because of immigration.'

- 2005 BBC Multiculturalism Survey
- 2008 Ipsos MORI survey

Agree: 12%, 25%
Disagree: 86%, 73%
Don't know: 2%, 1%
Refused: 0%, 0%

How much tension, if any, do you think there is in Britain between people of different races and nationalities?

None at all 4%
Don't know 2%
Not very much 18%
A fair amount 52%
A great deal 24%

And how likely or unlikely do you think it is that this tension will result in violence?
Base: All who think there is at least some tension (944)

Certain not to 2%
Don't know 2%
Very unlikely 8%
Certain to 9%
Very likely 17%
Fairly unlikely 25%
Fairly likely 38%

Source: Ipsos MORI, 18 April 2008.

Discrimination undermines sense of belonging

Information from the Joseph Rowntree Foundation

A report published today (19 March) found that nearly half of minority ethnic residents, including Muslims, said they had experienced race discrimination and 30 per cent of recent Muslim migrants had experienced religious discrimination. This was cited as a key barrier to a sense of belonging in Britain.

The report – *Immigration, faith and cohesion* – published by the Joseph Rowntree Foundation, was written by a team at the Centre on Migration, Policy and Society (COMPAS) at Oxford University. It looked at what factors contribute to, or undermine, community cohesion in three urban areas in England with large migrant and Muslim populations.

Most migrants felt there was no conflict in having a sense of belonging to both Britain and their country of origin. 60 per cent of long-term Muslim residents born outside the UK said the people most important to them were in Britain.

Co-author Hiranthi Jayaweera from COMPAS said: 'Evidence suggests that it is discrimination and the perception of being unwelcome, rather than attachment to their country of origin, that reduces migrants' sense of belonging in Britain.'

99 per cent of recent Muslim migrants strongly emphasised democracy, justice and security as the top reasons for living in Britain. Researchers also found that Muslims and non-Muslims shared a common concern about the problems of crime, drugs and pollution in the areas where they lived.

A good introduction to life in Britain through established communities was found to be a key way in which Muslim migrants were helped to integrate with wider British society. In the areas studied, new migrants relied heavily on established Muslim communities for the support and advice they needed on first arriving in Britain. Recent migrants from non-Muslim backgrounds in these areas said they felt more isolated.

Co-author Tufyal Choudhury said: 'The report shows the importance of family and friends in providing support for new migrants. Consideration should be given to how the role of established communities can be enhanced within a broader strategy towards the induction of new migrants into employment and community life.'

The findings also challenge perceptions of Muslim women as being isolated from wider society. The researchers looked at how different groups interact with each other and found that Muslims, including women with family responsibilities, interacted with people from other religious and ethnic backgrounds in different settings, and broadened their social networks over time in the UK. Both new migrants and established residents emphasised the important role played by schools, colleges and work places in bringing local people together.

19 March 2008

⇨ The above press release is reprinted with kind permission from the Joseph Rowntree Foundation. Visit www.jrf.org.uk for more information.

© *Joseph Rowntree Foundation*

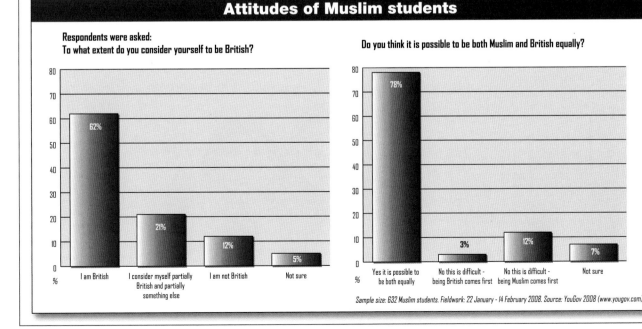

Attitudes of Muslim students

Respondents were asked:
To what extent do you consider yourself to be British?

- I am British — 62%
- I consider myself partially British and partially something else — 21%
- I am not British — 12%
- Not sure — 5%

Do you think it is possible to be both Muslim and British equally?

- Yes it is possible to be both equally — 78%
- No this is difficult - being British comes first — 3%
- No this is difficult - being Muslim comes first — 12%
- Not sure — 7%

Sample size: 632 Muslim students. Fieldwork: 22 January - 14 February 2008. Source: YouGov 2008 (www.yougov.com)

Diversity in primary schools promotes harmony

Information from the Economic and Social Research Council

For the first time, children as young as five have been shown to understand issues regarding integration and separation. The research, funded by the Economic and Social Research Council (ESRC), confirms that the ethnic composition of primary schools has a direct impact on children's attitudes towards those in other ethnic groups and on their ability to get on with their peers.

The research was a year-long longitudinal study with three sets of interviews at approximately six monthly intervals at 20 schools in Sussex and Kent. Teachers also participated by completing questionnaires. In all, 398 children took part in the study, 218 of these children were from ethnic minorities of whom the majority were of Indian origin. The ethnic minority composition of the schools ranged between 2% and 63%.

Highlighting the challenges faced by immigrant children, the study also showed that those attending schools characterised by higher ethnic diversity experienced fewer peer problems and less prejudice than those attending schools that are more homogeneous.

Researchers from the Universities of Sussex and Kent interviewed children from ethnic minority groups about their attitudes towards themselves, their heritage, culture and their relationships with their peers.

The interviews revealed that the vast majority of children from immigrant backgrounds wanted to keep their ethnic identity including their language and religious customs but, at the same time, they were keen to adopt as many of the practices and values of the host society as possible. This preference, known as an integrationist orientation, was already clear in children as young as five years old but was even more marked in the older age groups (8-11 years).

The research showed that having this integrationist attitude helped children both emotionally and socially: at the start of the study, the researchers found that minority children, particularly first generation immigrants, generally had lower self-esteem and were less well accepted by their peers than their white English classmates. But, when interviewed six and twelve months later, children with an integrationist orientation showed significant improvements in both these measures.

On the other hand, the researchers also found some evidence suggesting that constantly balancing the demands of their heritage culture with those of the host society took its toll. Professor Rupert Brown, who led the study, said: 'teachers' observations revealed that children with an integrationist outlook, particularly those who were first generation immigrants, were more likely to be 'teary' and show other symptoms of social anxiety than children who were solely focused on their own heritage. These children also reported more incidences of racial discrimination.'

These adverse effects were less common in immigrant children attending schools with a relatively high level of ethnic diversity than in those attending schools with a lower proportion of pupils from ethnic minorities. Indeed, according to Professor Brown, schools characterised by high ethnic diversity had clear social benefits for children regardless of their ethnic background:

'We found that, when the proportion of ethnic minority children in a school is at least 20%, both ethnic minority children and majority children tended to have higher self-esteem, children had more friendships with children from other ethnic groups, and there were fewer problems with peer relationships such as bullying.'

Professor Brown concludes: 'our findings add to a growing body of evidence suggesting that the more contact children have with other ethnic groups, the more cross-group friendships they will have and the less prejudiced they will be.' This argues against policies leading to reductions in school diversity such as the promotion of single faith schools.

24 July 2008

⇨ The above information is reprinted with kind permission from the Economic and Social Research Council. Visit www.esrcsocietytoday.ac.uk for more information.

© Economic and Social Research Council

Education the solution to racism

Information from YouthNet

Research launched today by online charity YouthNet to coincide with European Youth Week (2-9 November 2008), suggests that young people in the UK believe our multicultural society and having friends from other cultures makes the country a better place.

Two-thirds (63%) of respondents said that having a multicultural society makes the UK a better place

---

Three-quarters (72%) of the young people surveyed had friends from different countries or ethnic backgrounds and over half (55%) of all respondents welcomed this as an opportunity to learn about different cultures and expand their minds and experiences. Two-thirds (63%) of respondents said that having a multicultural society makes the UK a better place.

However, almost half (46%) agreed that racial tension in the UK was getting worse and three-quarters (69%) believed there was a general lack of awareness about other cultures in the UK. The majority (82%) of the young people surveyed thought that children should be taught about different cultures in school.

The research, which explored 841 young British people's attitudes towards diversity in the UK and European citizenship, as well as inter-cultural issues such as immigration and racism, was funded by the Youth in Action Programme and co-ordinated by the British Council.

Chief Executive of young people's charity YouthNet, Fiona Dawe, said: 'In this report, young people's views on Europe – and on race, immigration and multiculturalism in the UK today make interesting and encouraging reading, since for the most part they feel optimistic and open-minded about the UK's multicultural society and the possibilities for the future of the UK's relationship with Europe.'

In addition to the survey, the charity carried out a series of focus group sessions and, in-line with the survey results, many of the young people who took part felt that multiculturalism was part of British culture, with descriptions of 'Britishness' including 'flexible and all-embracing' and a 'morphing melting pot of culture and ideals'.

Like the survey respondents, the focus group members blamed a lack of understanding and education on the perceived increasing racial tension in the UK, and listed education and schools, as well as more balanced media coverage, as the key components in addressing racial tension and encouraging integration between different communities in the UK.

⇨ The above information is re-printed with kind permission from YouthNet. Visit www.youthnet.org for more information.

© YouthNet

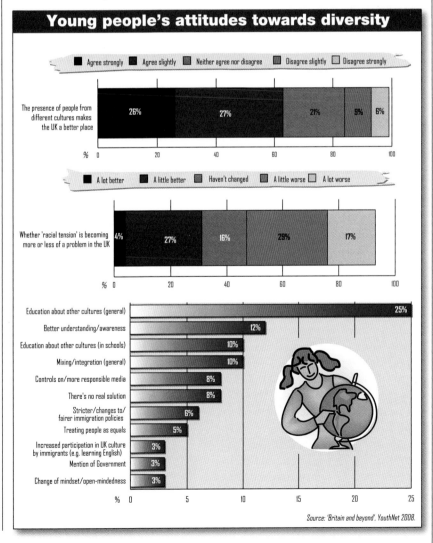

Young people's attitudes towards diversity

Source: 'Britain and beyond', YouthNet 2008.

Images of Islam in the UK

Two-thirds of newspaper stories say British Muslims are 'a threat' or 'problem'

A new report has found that, since 2000, two-thirds of newspaper articles about Muslims in Britain portray British Muslims as either 'a threat' or 'problem' and increasingly utilise negative and stereotypical imagery.

The 40-page report, entitled *Images of Islam in the UK*, set out to analyse a representative sample of newspaper articles in British tabloids and broadsheets between 2000 and 2008. In particular the authors, the Cardiff School of Journalism, Media and Cultural Studies, sought to engage with the 'routine, everyday coverage of British Muslims' over and above the coverage which occurred around key events, such as 11 September 2001 attacks and 7 July 2005 London bombings.

A growing focus

Coverage of British Muslims was shown to have increased significantly year on year, and by 2006 had reached a level 12 times higher than that in 2000. In both 2007 and 2008 coverage continued above 2005 rates, although it had dipped slightly from the peak in 2006. The authors describe how this coverage generated a momentum all of its own, 'lasting well beyond and independent of' the newsworthy events of 2001 and 2005.

Consistently negative 'news hook'

At the same time, the report found that the context in which British Muslims were portrayed was of a consistently negative nature. The main focus, or 'news hook', for a third of stories on British Muslims was either terrorism or the 'war on terror' over the period of the survey, whilst religious and cultural stories highlighting the cultural differences between British Muslims and other British people amounted to 22 per cent. 11 per cent of all stories focused on Muslim extremism. In stark contrast, only five per cent of all

By Rebecca Wood

stories covered 'attacks on or problems for British Muslims' and 'the notion of Islamophobia scarcely featured as a news topic'.

A significant yet subtle shift in story focus involves the steady increase in the proportion of stories which focus on religious and cultural differences, to such a degree that by 2008 these stories had overtaken terrorism as the single largest subject matter. It could be argued that this change in focus reflects the shift in British government policy, under the cloak of the 'community cohesion' framework, which quietly insinuates that 'British' and 'Muslim' are mutually exclusive identities.

The knock-on effect is that coverage of stories about anti-Muslim racism and attacks on British Muslims are elbowed out: from ten per cent in 2000 to only one per cent in 2008.

Pervasive cultural stereotyping

The report found that four of the five most common story threads associated Islam and/or Muslims 'with threats, problems or in opposition to dominant British values' whilst only two per cent of these stories suggested 'that Muslims supported dominant moral values'. In particular, the report highlights a number of stories which frame Britain as 'becoming a place of Muslim-only, "no-go" areas, where churches were being replaced by mosques, and Sharia law would soon be implemented'.

This insidious perception of Islam as a threat or a problem was further enhanced by the choice of descriptive language in the articles surveyed: the most common nouns employed in relation to Islam or Muslims were 'terrorist' or 'extremist' whilst the most widely used adjectives included 'fanatical', 'fundamentalist', 'radical' and 'militant'. In all, 'references to radical Muslims outnumber references to moderate Muslims by 17 to 1'. This choice of descriptive language was consistently used by both broadsheet and tabloid newspapers.

'Single Muslim male' or 'unidentified male Muslim group'

The newspaper articles surveyed also

appeared to rely on a stock set of images: that of the 'single Muslim male' or 'a group of unidentified Muslim men', often portrayed as either praying or preaching. The insinuation behind these portrayals of groups of Muslim men is, states the report, that they are 'the object of rather than the source of statements'. Moreover, 'a group of unidentified Muslim men is seen as an image that "speaks for itself": British Muslims are portrayed as one undifferentiated mass.

Islamophobic discourse

A recent report by the Institute of Race Relations, entitled *Integration, Islamophobia and civil rights in Europe*, concluded that the presence of an Islamophobic discourse across Europe was 'the primary barrier to integration'. This discourse was, the report found, constructed and disseminated 'by political parties, the media and the "liberati" in pursuit of an assimilationist agenda'. The findings of the Cardiff School of Journalism, Media and Cultural Studies complement and support these conclusions.

Images of Islam in the UK makes for a stimulating and thought-provoking read. It is delicately argued and convincingly supported by a powerful body of evidence, and effectively demonstrates the degree to which the portrayal of British Muslims in the print media has been hijacked by an Islamophobic climate, which resorts to lazy racial stereotyping and the repetition of negative and damaging stock stories.

The Institute of Race Relations is precluded from expressing a corporate view: any opinions expressed are therefore those of the authors.
9 September 2008

⇨ This first appeared on IRR News, a free service from the Institute of Race Relations. You can sign up to receive IRR News at www.irr.org. uk/subscribe. Teaching materials on black history, racism and anti-racism (including free downloadable teaching modules and a new DVD on struggles for black community) are available from the Institute of Race Relations, visit www.irr.org.uk/ publication.

© *Institute of Race Relations*

Contribution of faith communities

Information from ippr

Religion and faith communities play an important role in the cultural and social fabric of the UK, but public authorities need to do more to improve their understanding of the contribution they make, argues a new publication, *Faith in the Nation: Religion, identity and the public realm in Britain today*, released in December 2008 by the Institute for Public Policy Research (ippr).

Publishing a unique collection of essays from leading figures of the five largest faith communities in the UK, ippr argues that religion and faith play an increasingly important role in British society.

ippr argues that recognising and valuing the role of religion in British society needs to be balanced against a recognition of the core principles of British democracy – the equality of all before the law, the possession of citizenship rights irrespective of race, religion, gender and sexuality, and the rights of non-believers. The collection shows that British culture has provided a receptive home for members of different religious communities. Its underlying values of equal respect, pluralism and tolerance have made the UK a successful example of a multi-faith society.

In their essays, the faith leaders agree that Britishness and faith identity can be mutually reinforcing, and offer some sharp criticisms of patterns of cultural segregation.

Writing the foreword, Prime Minister Gordon Brown, says:

'Britain, of course, has a strong Christian tradition, but the landscape of our country today is resolutely multi-faith. Religious leaders writing here... raise some important questions about what the relationship between faith communities and the state should look like in a multi-faith society... How can we recognise and value the role of religion in British society without compromising the essential equalities that lie at the heart of the secular state?

'These questions and many others are explored in the pages of this groundbreaking publication – the first of its kind to bring faith leaders together to reflect on the kind of society that, as a nation, we aspire to build. Their answers today are not always the same, but one message comes across clearly and consistently: that religious belief will continue to be an important component of our shared British identity as it evolves and that British society can and does draw strength from its diverse faith communities.'

Although different ideas and views are explored and expressed by the faith leaders in their essays, some notable common themes emerge. Specifically, the belief that despite some struggles to be accepted, their faiths have become part of the fabric of Britain and that their communities have made important contributions to British society. Each of them points to ways in which their religions have been shaped by their interaction with British culture and values.

The contributors also identify some common challenges, specifically, the need for a policy to move beyond a static and segregated notion of multiculturalism, by articulating a stronger common sense of British identity. Britishness, they argue, can act as a bridge between the legitimate claims of faith identities and a common shared set of national loyalties, which are essential for promoting social solidarity and community cohesion.
8 December 2008

⇨ The above information is reprinted with kind permission from ippr. Visit www.ippr.org for more information.

© *ippr*

⇨ About half (49%) of the general public are optimistic Britain will be a more tolerant society in ten years' time. (page 3)

⇨ Three in five (60%) of the general population and two in three (66%) of those in ethnic minority groups think religion is more divisive than race today. (page 3)

⇨ Almost 20 per cent of children under the age of 16 are from an ethnic minority and nearly ten per cent of children live in a family with a multiple white, black or Asian heritage. (page 6)

⇨ Stop and search figures for London between January and March 2007 showed that a black person is four times more likely to be stopped and searched than a white person and three times more likely to be arrested. (page 7)

⇨ In 2007-08 police recorded 4,823 racially or religiously motivated crimes in which somebody was injured, 4,320 crimes without injury, and 26,495 cases of harassment. (page 9)

⇨ A new report from the Runnymede Trust has identified different approaches to reporting of crime dependent on whether the victim or perpetrator are black or white. The authors argue that these approaches serve to influence public opinion and policy, and contribute to the reinforcement of racist stereotypes. (page 10)

⇨ Academically able Black Caribbean pupils are less likely to be entered for higher-tier maths and science tests than white children with the same achievement record, a University of Warwick study has found. (page 14)

⇨ Among girls, 85 per cent of white pupils want to stay on at school at age 16, compared with 94 per cent of ethnic Pakistani and Bangladeshi pupils, 95 per cent of ethnic Indian and Black Caribbean pupils and 99 per cent of Black African pupils. (page 15)

⇨ The 1976 Race Relations Act makes it unlawful for an employer to discriminate against you on racial grounds. Race includes colour, nationality, ethnic or national origins. (page 16)

⇨ A new Equality Bill, expected to come into force in 2010, will allow businesses to favour recruiting under-represented groups to their workforce if there was a choice between two equally qualified individuals, one from a minority group and one from an over-represented group. (page 19)

⇨ Black Caribbean men are still more than three times as likely to be unemployed as white men. (page 21)

⇨ Research from the University of Bristol shows that Gypsy and Traveller communities in Britain experience extensive inequalities, including pervasive racism and discrimination. (page 23)

⇨ A survey by the Pew Research Centre has found increasing levels of anti-Semitism across Europe, with particularly strong negativity in Spain, Poland and Russia. The survey also revealed strong anti-Muslim views in those three countries, as well as in Germany and France. (page 24)

⇨ A study from the Runnymede Trust has concluded that the white working class are discriminated against on a range of different fronts, but they are not discriminated against because they are white. (page 25)

⇨ 48 per cent of Black Caribbean men and 34 per cent of Black Caribbean women are in mixed-race relationships. (page 30)

⇨ Professor Ludi Simpson and Dr Nissa Finney from the University of Manchester have found no evidence 'whatsoever' for the existence of race ghettos in the UK. In fact, they claim the opposite is true, with increasing ethnic mixing. (page 33)

⇨ In a survey by Ipsos MORI, 24% of those questioned believed that there was a 'great deal' of tension between people of different races and nationalities and 52% said they believed there was a 'fair amount' of tension. Only four per cent thought there was no tension at all. (page 34)

⇨ A report from the Joseph Rowntree Foundation found that nearly half of minority ethnic residents, including Muslims, said they had experienced race discrimination and 30 per cent of recent Muslim migrants had experienced religious discrimination. (page 35)

⇨ Research funded by the Economic and Social Research Council (ESRC) confirms that the ethnic composition of primary schools has a direct impact on children's attitudes towards those in other ethnic groups and on their ability to get on with their peers. (page 36)

⇨ Three-quarters (72%) of young people surveyed by YouthNet had friends from different countries or ethnic backgrounds and two-thirds (63%) of respondents said that having a multicultural society makes the UK a better place. (page 37)

⇨ A new report has found that, since 2000, two-thirds of newspaper articles about Muslims in Britain portray British Muslims as either 'a threat' or 'problem' and increasingly utilise negative and stereotypical imagery. (page 38)

GLOSSARY

Anti-Semitism
Discrimination against or hostility towards Jewish people.

Assimilation
Cultural assimilation is when individuals adopt some or all aspects of a dominant culture, such as its religion, language and values.

Black History Month
A celebration and remembrance of the contributions and achievements of the black and minority ethnic people as part of our shared history. In the UK, Black History Month is celebrated in October.

Discrimination
To treat one group of people less favourably than others because of their race, colour, nationality, or ethnic or national origin. Direct discrimination occurs when race, colour, nationality or ethnic or national origin is used as an explicit reason for discriminating. Indirect discrimination occurs when there are rules, regulations or procedures operating which have the effect of discriminating against certain groups of people.

Diversity
Accepting and respecting differences between and within different groups.

Equality Bill
The Equality Bill, expected to come into force in 2010, will allow businesses to favour recruiting under-represented groups if there is a choice between two equally qualified individuals, of whom one is from a minority group and one is from an over-represented group.

Hate crime
Hate crime is any criminal offence committed against a person or property motivated by an offender's hatred of someone because of their race, colour, ethnic origin, nationality or national origins, religion, gender or gender identity, sexual orientation or disability.

Institutional racism
When an organisation's procedures and policies disadvantage people from minority ethnic backgrounds. It is defined by the Stephen Lawrence Inquiry as 'the collective failure of an organisation to provide an appropriate and professional service to people because of their colour, culture or ethnic origin. It can be seen or detected in processes, attitudes and behaviour which amount to discrimination through unwitting prejudice, ignorance, thoughtlessness and racial stereotyping which disadvantages minority ethnic people.'

The Macpherson report
The publication of the Macpherson report in February 1999 followed a public inquiry (the Stephen Lawrence Inquiry) into the Metropolitan Police's investigation of the murder of black teenager Stephen Lawrence, who was fatally stabbed as he waited for a bus in April 1993. The Met's investigation of the murder had led to accusations of incompetence and racism. Sir William Macpherson's report identified 'institutional racism' within the Met and made recommendations aimed at improving police attitudes to race issues. No-one has ever been convicted of Stephen Lawrence's murder.

Multiculturalism
Multiculturalism is the right of groups and individuals to pursue their own cultural choices, heritage and faiths while respecting the rights of others to do the same.

Positive action
Refers to a range of measures that employers can legally take to help people from under-represented groups compete for jobs on equal terms with other applicants.

Race Relations Act
The 1976 Race Relations Act sets out the circumstances in which discrimination on the grounds of race is unlawful. It defines four types of discrimination: direct discrimination, indirect discrimination, victimisation and harassment.

The Racial and Religious Hatred Act
This law came into effect in 2007 and made it a criminal offence to use threatening words or behaviour with the intention of stirring up hatred against any group of people because of their religious beliefs or lack of beliefs.

Racism
Racism is the belief that people who have a different skin colour, nationality or culture are inferior. Racism can take many forms, ranging from verbal abuse to outright physical attacks on a person or property. Racism can also be non-verbal, for example denying a person from a minority ethnic background a job.

Rivers of Blood
The name given to a notorious speech made by Conservative politician Enoch Powell on 20 April 1968. He spoke about immigration, and his vision of the future if new anti-discrimination legislation were enacted by the Labour government in power at the time. Powell's views were highly controversial and he became one of the most loved and loathed politicians of his day.

Segregation
The separation of people from different ethnic groups.

INDEX

Additional Resources

Other Issues *titles*

If you are interested in researching further some of the issues raised in *Racial and Ethnic Discrimination* you may like to read the following titles in the **Issues** series:

➪ Vol. 175 *Citizenship and Participation* (ISBN 978 1 86168 489 9)

➪ Vol. 167 *Our Human Rights* (ISBN 978 1 86168 471 4)

➪ Vol. 165 *Bullying Issues* (ISBN 978 1 86168 469 1)

➪ Vol. 156 *Travel and Tourism* (ISBN 978 1 86168 443 1)

➪ Vol. 150 *Migration and Population* (ISBN 978 1 86168 423 3)

➪ Vol. 148 *Religious Beliefs* (ISBN 978 1 86168 421 9)

➪ Vol. 147 *The Terrorism Problem* (ISBN 978 1 86168 420 2)

➪ Vol. 142 *Media Issues* (ISBN 978 1 86168 408 0)

➪ Vol. 139 *The Education Problem* (ISBN 978 1 86168 391 5)

➪ Vol. 137 *Crime and Anti-Social Behaviour* (ISBN 978 1 86168 389 2)

➪ Vol. 107 *Work Issues* (ISBN 978 1 86168 327 4)

➪ Vol. 89 *Refugees* (ISBN 978 1 86168 290 1)

For more information about these titles, visit our website at www.independence.co.uk/publicationslist

Useful *organisations*

You may find the websites of the following organisations useful for further research:

➪ **Business in the Community:** www.bitc.org.uk

➪ **The Centre for Social Cohesion:** www.socialcohesion.co.uk

➪ **Colourful:** www.iamcolourful.com

➪ **Commission for Equality and Human Rights:** www.equalityhumanrights.com

➪ **Communities and Local Government:** www.communities.gov.uk

➪ **Economic and Social Research Council:** www.esrcsocietytoday.ac.uk

➪ **Equality Challenge Unit:** www.ecu.ac.uk

➪ **Institute for Public Policy Research:** www.ippr.org

➪ **Institute for Social & Economic Research:** www.iser.essex.ac.uk

➪ **Institute of Education:** www.ioe.ac.uk

➪ **The Institute of Race Relations:** www.irr.org.uk

➪ **Joseph Rowntree Foundation:** www.jrf.org.uk

➪ **The National Assembly Against Racism:** www.naar.org.uk

➪ **The National Youth Agency:** www.nya.org.uk

➪ **The Runnymede Trust:** www.runnymedetrust.org

➪ **Show Racism the Red Card:** www.srtrc.org

➪ **Your Rights:** www.yourrights.org.uk

➪ **YouthNet:** www.youthnet.org

ACKNOWLEDGEMENTS

The publisher is grateful for permission to reproduce the following material.

While every care has been taken to trace and acknowledge copyright, the publisher tenders its apology for any accidental infringement or where copyright has proved untraceable. The publisher would be pleased to come to a suitable arrangement in any such case with the rightful owner.

Chapter One: Racial Discrimination

Frequently asked questions, © Show Racism the Red Card, *Public attitudes to race and religion in Britain*, © Ipsos MORI, *What is race discrimination?*, © Liberty, *Institutions must catch up with public on race issues*, © Equality and Human Rights Commission, *Race equality in the UK*, © Colourful, *Racism*, © NSPCC, *Hate crime*, © Crown copyright is reproduced with the permission of Her Majesty's Stationery Office, *Press reporting of violent crime fuels racism*, © Runnymede Trust, *Say what you like, we have to get past this 'humour'*, © The Scotsman, *Whatever happened to free speech?*, © Telegraph Group Limited, *Higher-tier test entry for Black Caribbean pupils*, © University of Warwick, *White children have lower educational aspirations*, © University of Bristol, *Religion and nationality – the new 'race'?*, © Institute of Education, *Racial discrimination at work*, © Crown copyright is reproduced with the permission of Her Majesty's Stationery Office, *Race inequality increasing in the UK workforce*, © Business in the Community, *Equality Bill criticised by employers as unrealistic*, © Reed Business Information, *New plans for achieving race equality in the UK*, © Crown copyright is reproduced with the permission of Her Majesty's Stationery Office, *Is Black History Month still relevant?*, © The National Youth Agency, *Gypsies and Travellers experience racism*, © University of Bristol, *Rise in anti-Jewish and anti-Muslim attitudes in Europe*, © The Centre for Social Cohesion, *Rise in anti-Semitic attacks*, © Guardian News and Media Limited, *Britain's forgotten race victims?*, © Runnymede Trust.

Chapter Two: Ethnicity and Identity

Multiculturalism – a cause for celebration, © National Assembly Against Racism, *Cultural identity*, © Parentline Plus, *Society damaged by policies on multiculturalism*, © Telegraph Group Limited, *Second generation*, © Crown copyright is reproduced with the permission of Her Majesty's Stationery Office, *The rise of mixed-race Britain*, © Institute for Social & Economic Research, *I have no doubt what colour I am*, © Guardian News and Media Limited, *Letters: Identity is about more than black or white*, © Guardian News and Media Limited, *'Myths' threaten racial harmony*, © University of Manchester, *Rivers of blood survey*, © Ipsos MORI, *Discrimination undermines sense of belonging*, © Joseph Rowntree Foundation, *Diversity in primary schools promotes harmony*, © Economic and Social Research Council, *Education the solution to racism*, © YouthNet, *Images of Islam in the UK*, © Institute of Race Relations, *Contribution of faith communities*, © ippr.

Photographs

Flickr: page 27 (Melissa Rudick).
Stock Xchng: pages 4 (Robbie Owen-Wahl); 9 (Jason Antony); 15 (renata jun); 29 (ophelia cherry).
Wikimedia Commons: page 32 (United States Senate).

Illustrations

Pages 1, 11, 22, 31: Angelo Madrid; pages 5, 13, 26, 33: Don Hatcher; pages 6, 20, 28, 38: Simon Kneebone; pages 17, 36: Bev Aisbett.

Editorial and layout by Claire Owen, on behalf of Independence Educational Publishers.

And with thanks to the team: Mary Chapman, Sandra Dennis, Claire Owen and Jan Sunderland.

Lisa Firth
Cambridge
May, 2009